MARY FORD
CHILDREN'S
BIRTHDAY
CAKES

MARY FORD
CHILDREN'S BIRTHDAY CAKES

MARY FORD

A MARY FORD BOOK

Published 1994 by Mary Ford Publications Limited,
99 Spring Road, Tyseley, Birmingham B11 3DJ England.

Typesetting by Alexander Print & Production, Poole.
Printed and bound by BPC Paulton Books Ltd.
ISBN 0 946429 46 4

THE AUTHOR

Mary Ford's abilities and skills as a cake decorator have ensured her a place as one of the country's leading cake decorators. Her step-by-step teaching method is known to thousands of cake decorating enthusiasts from all over the world, many of whom owe their abiding interest in the art to Mary.

However, Mary's appeal is not limited to cake decorating enthusiasts. Her personal warmth and simplicity of style have endeared her to two generations of busy mothers and aspiring decorators seeking inspiration and instruction. Mary is never too busy to answer a query personally, and she supervises every stage of her books, ensuring that her enthusiasm and dedication to her craft emanate from every page.

She is helped in this work by her husband Michael, the editorial director and photographer for all the Mary Ford books, who shares Mary's dedication to bringing the pleasure of cake decoration to an ever increasing audience.

Mary Ford acknowledges with grateful thanks the assistance of Mary Smith and Dawn Pennington in creating some of the items and cakes featured in this book.

ACKNOWLEDGEMENTS

Cakeboards Limited, 47-53 Dace Road, London, E3 2NH. Manufacturers and suppliers of cake decorating equipment and decorations to the wholesale and retail trade.

Orchard Products, 51 Hallyburton Road, Hove, East Sussex, BN3 7GP. Manufacturers and suppliers of cake decorating equipment to the retail trade by mail order.

Prestige, 23-26 High Street, Egham, Surrey, for the supply of cake tins and cookware used in this book.

CONTENTS

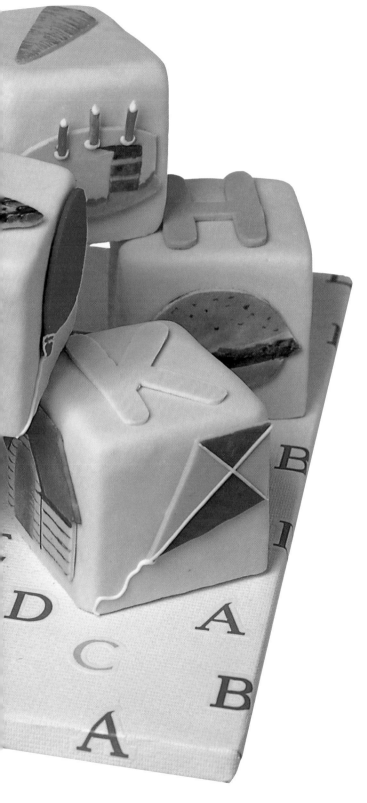

NOTE: WHEN MAKING ANY OF THE RECIPES IN
THIS BOOK, FOLLOW ONE SET OF MEASUREMENTS
ONLY AS THEY ARE NOT INTERCHANGEABLE.

INTRODUCTION

Making children's cakes is fun! Anyone can do it with this simple, fully illustrated step-by-step guide.

In response to numerous requests from decorators of all ages and experience, I have created fifty-five brand new, innovative designs for children's cakes, many of which are suitable for beginners. As a base, I have used the sponge cakes that appeal to children, with easy to apply, and sweet-tasting, butter icing or sugarpaste coatings and decorations. Sugarpaste is such an easy medium to work in, children themselves will enjoy helping to create their favourite characters.

Cake decorating is an exciting and rewarding hobby which brings pleasure to both the recipient and the decorator. Nowhere is this more apparent than in making children's cakes. The joy that a child has in seeing a cake that has been specially made just for them is well worth the time and effort involved. Not that all cakes need great effort. It is possible to create stunning cakes with very little time and skill. If time is limited, many of the items required can be purchased, including ready-made sugarpaste and instant royal icing (just add water).

As usual, the book opens with tried and tested recipes for perfect cakes and decorating mediums. For the first time I have included an extremely adaptable, and delicious, Madeira-type cake which cuts well and holds its texture. This cake incorporates ground rice and makes unusual shapes and cut-outs very simple to create. It can be coloured and flavoured, chocolate being a favourite, or have cherries, nuts and fruit added. It makes a wonderful light fruit cake that can be butter iced or sugarpaste coated.

Each completed cake is fully illustrated, and colour photographs highlight every stage of the decorating process. The introductory section and glossary provide an instant reference for techniques and terms.

A wide variety of cakes are presented, based on storybook and nursery rhyme characters, appealing animals and mythological creatures. Cakes have been designed which will fit in with a 'theme' party and children could be invited to dress accordingly. Pirates and Snow White and her friends have perennial appeal but children will enjoy exercising their imagination to create newer characters from their favourite video, television show, book, or comic. Small cakes and decorations can be used as presents to take home from a party.

Some cakes can be adapted to suit the particular child's interests. The nurse on page seventy four can easily become a cook, fireman, footballer, etc. Similarly, 'Andy' on page eighty nine can become any name by adapting the shape of the first letter and making sugarpaste cut-outs as required.

I feel sure that all the designs will fire your imagination and, especially if this is your first venture into cake decorating, will bring you many happy and rewarding hours.

EQUIPMENT

Before commencing work, gather together all the equipment you will need. All equipment should be scrupulously clean and free from grease. An electric mixer saves a great deal of time and energy, but is not essential for success.

You will find that many of the items needed for cake decorating can already be found in the kitchen or can be improvised if necessary. However, if you are buying equipment, do buy the best quality available as, with care, this should last a lifetime.

Where possible, keep decorating utensils for this job only as icing and sugarpaste can easily become tainted or discoloured by food particles, odours, grease or rust. Food approved plastic, stainless steel and glass bowls are ideal and cake tins should be strong and rigid.

You will need a heavy, smooth rolling pin for sugarpaste and nylon spacers make achieving an even thickness much easier. Spacers can also be used for marking the paste, as can clean steel or plastic rulers, but any straight plastic edge of appropriate thickness will do.

A selection of stainless steel palette knives will be required for mixing-in and coating cakes. An 18cm (7in) and a 10cm (4in) should be sufficient for all tasks. A fork or the end of a paintbrush is useful for creating textures and shapes, as is a modelling tool, but any suitably shaped implement can be used to improvise.

Piping tube shapes required are illustrated in the glossary. Piping tubes can be plastic or metal. It is important to wash out piping tubes immediately after use to prevent the icing hardening inside.

Some cakes require a crimper, which can be purchased from a cake-craft shop, but any design of crimper can be used according to what is available. Plastic dowel can also be purchased from a cake-craft supplier, as can a ready-made piping bag in nylon or paper and confectioners dusting powder and food approved colours. Most supermarkets also stock food approved colours and ready-made sugarpaste and instant royal icing.

Cake boards are important. Always use the thicker type of the stipulated size to hold the cake. Card cards, which are much thinner, are not suitable for supporting weight. Cake boards can be covered in decorative paper, but this should be food-approved or should be covered in non-stick paper or a small cake card. A cake should never be placed directly onto a non-food-approved covering.

A fine sponge is useful for creating texture. The type used in the bathroom is ideal, as long as it is fresh and clean. Sponges used for other purposes should be avoided.

A turntable makes decorating much easier but this is not essential as it can be improvised by an upturned plate or cake tin. A good turntable is large and solid enough to support a heavy cake, with a minimum diameter of 23cm (9in). It should have a non-slip base and be easy to turn.

ALL-IN-ONE SPONGE CAKE

This sponge is ideal for birthday cakes and cutting into shapes for novelty cakes.

SPONGE TIN SHAPES		SPONGE TIN SIZES				
ROUND	15cm (6in)	18cm (7in)	20.5cm (8in)	23cm (9in)	25.5cm (10in)	28cm (11in)
SQUARE	12.5cm (5in)	15cm (6in)	18cm (7in)	20.5cm (8in)	23cm (9in)	25.5cm (10in)
PUDDING BASIN	450ml (¾pt)	600ml (1pt)	750ml (1¼pt)	900ml (1½pt)	1 litre (1¾pt)	1.2 Litre (2pt)
LOAF TIN		18.5 x 9 x 5cm 450g (1lb)			21.5 x 11 x 6cm 900g (2lb)	
Self-raising flour	45g (1½oz)	60g (2oz)	85g (3oz)	115g (4oz)	170g (6oz)	225g (8oz)
Baking powder	¼tsp	½tsp	¾tsp	1tsp	1½tsp	2tsp
Soft (tub) margarine	45g (1½oz)	60g (2oz)	85g (3oz)	115g (4oz)	170g (6oz)	225g (8oz)
Caster sugar	45g (1½oz)	60g (2oz)	85g (3oz)	115g (4oz)	170g (6oz)	225g (8oz)
Eggs	1 size 4	1 size 3	1 size 1	2 size 3	3 size 3	4 size 3
Baking temperature		---------------- 170°C (325°F) or Gas Mark 3 ----------------------------				
Approximate baking time	20 min	25 mins	30 mins	32 mins	35 mins	40 mins

PLEASE NOTE: Baking times for sponges baked in pudding basins and loaf tins may take longer.

BAKING TEST: When the sponge has reached the recommended baking time, open the oven door slowly and, if the sponge is pale in colour, continue baking until light brown. When light brown, run your fingers across the top gently and the sponge should spring back when touched. If not then continue baking and test every few minutes.

STORAGE: When cold the sponge can be deep-frozen for up to six months. Use within three days of baking or defrosting.

PORTIONS: A 20.5cm (8in) round sponge should provide approximately sixteen portions when decorated.

For chocolate flavoured sponges:

For every 115g (4oz) of flour used in the recipe add the following ingredients: 2tbsp of cocoa powder dissolved in 2tbsp of hot water, leave to cool then add to the other ingredients in step 3.

For coffee flavoured sponges:

For every 115g (4oz) of flour used in the recipe add 2tsp of instant coffee dissolved in 1tbsp of boiling water, leave to cool then add to the other ingredients in step 3.

For orange or lemon flavoured sponges:

For every 115g (4oz) of flour used in the recipe add the grated rind of one orange or lemon to the other ingredients in step 3.

INGREDIENTS *for Two 20.5cm (8in) round sponges*
(see opposite page for additional sizes)

170g self-raising flour (6oz)
1½ tsp baking powder
170g soft (tub) margarine (6oz)
170g caster sugar (6oz)
3 eggs, size 3

BAKING

Bake in a pre-heated oven at 170°C (325°F) or
Gas Mark 3 for approximately 30 minutes.

EQUIPMENT

Two 20.5cm round sponge tins (8in)
OR two 18cm square sponge tins (7in)
Soft (tub) margarine for greasing
Brush
Greaseproof paper
Mixing bowl
Sieve
Beater
Spatula

1 Grease the tins with soft (tub) margarine, line the bases with greaseproof paper then grease the paper.

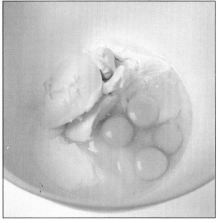

2 Sift the flour and baking powder together twice to ensure a thorough mix. Then place into a mixing bowl with all the other ingredients.

3 Beat mixture for 3-4 minutes until light in colour.

4 Spread the mixture evenly between the two tins. Bake in pre-heated oven (see baking test).

5 When the sponges are baked, leave to cool in the tins for 5 minutes, then carefully turn out onto a wire tray until cold.

6 When cold, sandwich the sponges together with jam and cream then place into a refrigerator for 1 hour before decorating.

MADEIRA SPONGE CAKE

This cake has a firm texture which is ideal for cutting. Children particularly like the taste as it is not as rich as a filled sponge. The cake is versatile and lends itself to the addition of cherries, nuts, sultanas, chopped bananas or chocolate (cocoa powder or chocolate chips) to vary the texture and taste.

SPONGE TIN SHAPES				SPONGE TIN SIZES			
ROUND	15cm (6in)	18cm (7in)	20.5cm (8in)	23cm (9in)	25.5cm (10in)	28cm (11in)	30.5cm (12in)
SQUARE	12.5cm (5in)	15cm (6in)	18cm (7in)	20.5cm (8in)	23cm (9in)	25.5cm (10in)	28cm (11in)
Butter or margarine	115g (4oz)	170g (6oz)	225g (8oz)	285g (10oz)	340g (12oz)	400g (14oz)	450g (16oz)
Caster sugar	85g (3oz)	130g (4½oz)	170g (6oz)	225g (8oz)	255g (9oz)	295g (10½oz)	340g (12oz)
Self raising flour	145g (5oz)	215g (7½oz)	285g (10oz)	370g (13oz)	425g (15oz)	495g (17½oz)	570g (20oz)
Ground rice	85g (3oz)	130g (4½oz)	170g (6oz)	225g (8oz)	255g (9oz)	295g (10½oz)	340g (12oz)
Eggs, size 2	1½	2½	3	4	4½	5½	6)
Fresh milk	70g (2½oz)	130g (4½oz)	145g (5oz)	225g (8oz)	255g (9oz)	270g (9½oz)	285g (10oz)
Baking temperature	---------------------------- 170°C (325°F) or Gas Mark 3 ------------------------------						
Approximate baking time	40mins	1hr	1¼ hrs	----------------- 1½hrs to 1¾hrs -------------			

BAKING TEST: Bring the cake forward in the oven at the end of the recommended baking time so that it can be tested. Insert a stainless steel skewer into the centre of the cake and slowly withdraw it. If the cake is sufficiently baked, the skewer will come out as cleanly as it went in. Continue baking at the same temperature if the cake mixture clings to the skewer. Test every ten minutes until the skewer is clean when withdrawn from the cake.

STORAGE: When cold a madeira sponge cake can be deep frozen for up to six months. Use within three days of baking or defrosting.

PORTIONS: A 20.5cm (8in) round madeira sponge cake should serve approximately sixteen portions when decorated.

For chocolate flavoured sponge cake:
For every 225g (8oz) butter used, substitute 2tbsp of cocoa powder for 1 tbsp flour and 1 tbsp ground rice.

1 Grease the tin lightly with butter. Fully line tin with greaseproof paper, then grease the paper.

INGREDIENTS *for an 18cm square cake tin (7in) or 20.5cm round cake tin (8in)*

225g butter (8oz)
170g caster sugar (6oz)
285g self raising flour (10oz)
170g ground rice (6oz)
3 eggs, size 2
145g fresh milk (5oz)

EQUIPMENT

Greaseproof paper
Mixing bowl
Mixing spoon
Spatula

BAKING

Bake in a pre-heated oven at 170°C (325°F) or Gas Mark 3 for approximately 1¼ hours

2 Cream the butter and sugar together until light and fluffy. Beat in half the egg.

3 Mix together the remaining egg and the milk. Then mix into the batter alternately with the sieved flour and ground rice.

4 Place mixture in the tin and, using a spatula, level the top.

5 Bake in pre-heated oven for the recommended time and then test. When baked, leave in the tin to cool for ten minutes before turning out onto a wire rack to cool completely.

SWISS ROLL

INGREDIENTS

85g soft (tub) margarine (3oz)
170g caster sugar (6oz)
3 eggs, size 3
170g self-raising flour, sifted (6oz)

EQUIPMENT

33 x 23cm swiss roll tin (13 x 9in)
Greaseproof paper
Mixing bowl
Beater
Cranked (step) palette knife
Damp tea towel
Caster sugar for dusting

Bake in pre-heated oven at 200°C (400°F) or Gas Mark 6, for 10-12 minutes on the middle shelf.

For chocolate swiss roll:
Dissolve 3 level tbsp of cocoa powder in 3tbsp hot water, leave to cool and add to the above ingredients.

Suggested fillings:
Butter icing with the addition of any of the following: melted chocolate, chopped nuts, fresh lemon or orange, chopped glacé fruits.

1 Grease the swiss roll tin with melted margarine, line with greaseproof paper then grease the paper.

2 Place all the ingredients into a mixing bowl and beat for 2-3 minutes or until well mixed.

3 Spread mixture into the tin evenly. Whilst baking place greaseproof paper, slightly larger than the tin, onto a damp tea-towel.

4 Dredge the paper with caster sugar. When baked, immediately turn out the sponge onto the paper, then remove the baking paper.

5 Leave to cool for a few minutes, spread filling over the top. See opposite page if using butter icing.

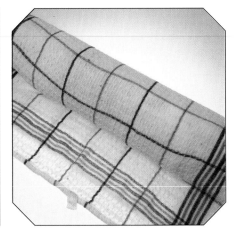

6 Immediately roll up the sponge and keep tightly covered with the damp cloth until cold. Then remove cloth and paper.

BUTTER ICING and FUDGE ICING

BUTTER ICING

INGREDIENTS

115g butter, at room temperature
(4oz)
170-225g icing sugar, sifted (6-8oz)
Few drops vanilla extract
1-2tbsp milk

This recipe can be flavoured and
coloured as desired.

1 For the butter icing: beat the butter until light and fluffy.

2 Beat in the icing sugar, a little at a time, adding the vanilla extract and sufficient milk to give a fairly firm but spreading consistency.

FUDGE ICING

INGREDIENTS

200g icing sugar (7oz)
30g golden syrup (1oz)
1½tbsp milk
45g butter (1½oz)

Fudge icing can be used as frosting
or filling, coating cakes and piping.
It can also be frozen and stored in a
refrigerator until required.

1 For the fudge icing: sift the icing sugar into a bowl. Then put the remaining ingredients into a small saucepan and stir over low heat until the butter has melted.

2 Bring to almost boiling then immediately pour the mixture into the icing sugar.

3 Stir until smooth. Follow the suggestions for the various uses of this fudge icing.

SUGARPASTE

INGREDIENTS

2tbsp cold water
1½ level tsp powdered gelatine
1½ tbsp liquid glucose
2tsp glycerin

450g icing sugar, sifted (1lb)

MODELLING PASTE

Add 2tsp of gum tragacanth to the basic sugarpaste recipe and work well in.
Leave for 24 hours before use.
Store as sugarpaste.

COLOURING SUGARPASTE

Add food colour a little at a time and mix well in until the required colour is achieved. Always make sufficient coloured sugarpaste as it is difficult to match colour later.

MOTTLED SUGARPASTE

Partially mix food colouring into sugarpaste. Then roll out.

  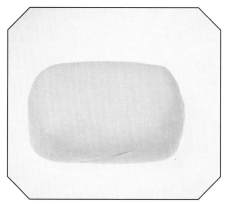

1 Pour the water into a saucepan and sprinkle on the powdered gelatine. Dissolve over low heat. Stir in the glucose and glycerin then remove from the heat.

2 Gradually add and stir in the icing sugar with a spoon to avoid making a lumpy mixture. When unable to stir anymore icing sugar into mixture, turn out onto table.

3 Mix in the remaining icing sugar using fingers then knead until a pliable smooth paste is formed. Store in a sealed container until required.

COVERING CAKES

 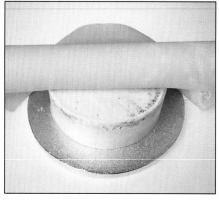 

1 Coat the cake-side and top with a thin layer of butter icing. Chill for 1 hour in the refrigerator.

2 When chilled, roll out the sugarpaste and place over the cake, using a rolling pin.

3 Smooth the paste over the top, then down the side, using palm of hand. Trim around the cake-base or board edge. Leave until dry before decorating.

ROYAL ICING

INGREDIENTS

100g fresh egg white, or
albumen solution (3½oz)
450g icing sugar, sifted (1lb)
If using fresh egg whites,
separate 24 hours before use.

COLOURING

Add food colour a little at a time
and mix well in until required
colour is achieved.

1 Pour the egg whites into a bowl.
Slowly mix in half the icing sugar
until dissolved.

2 Then slowly mix in the remaining
sugar. Run a spatula around the
inside of the bowl to ensure all the
ingredients are blended together.

3 Thoroughly beat mixture until light
and fluffy. Peaks should be formed
when the spoon or beater is lifted.
Clean down inside then cover with
a damp cloth until required.

HOW TO PIPE LINES

Always work so that you draw the piping bag towards
yourself with the bag aligned to the direction of
the stroke. To steady the tube, use both hands. Touch the
surface with the tube end, keeping piping bag at a shallow
angle. Squeeze piping bag until icing appears, then pipe and,
at the same time, lift the piping bag. Bring the piping bag
towards you. Before reaching
the end of the line, stop squeezing and lower piping bag to
the surface. To finish the line, touch the surface and pull
the tube away, keeping the piping bag upright. Strips of
food approved thin card can be used as a guide to keep the
work straight.

HOW TO PIPE SHAPES

Shells: Place the tube against the surface and press.
Continue pressing and start to lift the piping bag. With the
piping bag slowly moving upwards, continue pressing until
the size required is reached. Stop pressing, move the piping
bag down to the surface and pull away to complete the
shape.

Rope: Holding the piping bag at a low angle, pipe a spring
shape along the surface in a clockwise direction. Continue
piping until length required. Pull the piping bag away to
complete the shape.

Hints and tips

BAKING

Weigh all ingredients carefully, particularly when using the all-in-one recipe.

Never use eggs straight out of the refrigerator. Allow to reach room temperature.

All ingredients should preferably be at room temperature.

Always use the correct size tin for the amount of batter.

Cakes should be baked on the centre shelf of the oven unless specified.

CURDLING

Curdling can occur if eggs are added too quickly to the cake mixture or if there is insufficient beating between the additions. If curdling does occur, immediately beat in a small amount of flour until the batter is smooth and then continue adding egg, a little at a time.

BUTTER ICING

To obtain best results, always use fresh butter at a temperature of 18-21°C (65-70°F).

FUDGE ICING

When using the icing as a coating, pour over the cake as soon as it is made.

To use as a filling, allow the mixture to cool and beat well with a wooden spoon.

For piping, use when thick enough to hold its shape.

This icing can be stored in a refrigerator and melted again to a flowing consistency.

Chocolate fudge icing can be made by the addition of 20ml (2 heaped tsp) cocoa and 10ml (2tsp) hot water.

COLOURING and PAINTING

Add a little colour at a time when colouring sugarpaste or royal icing.

Most paste colours dry darker.

If mixing a large quantity, leave overnight to settle before use.

Always colour sufficient icing or sugarpaste to complete the decoration as it is virtually impossible to match the colour. Taste coloured sugarpaste or royal icing before use as too much colour will make it bitter.

Let sugarpaste dry thoroughly before painting.

When painting, use a very small amount of colour on the tip of a fine paintbrush.

To colour granulated sugar: place in a bowl, add a drop of colouring. Stir well with a spoon. Turn onto greaseproof paper to dry. Store in a jar.

SUGARPASTE

Sugarpaste can be purchased ready-made if required.

Sugarpaste should be made 24 hours before use.

If the paste is too dry, add a little white fat or egg white.

If the paste is too sticky, add a little cornflour or icing sugar.

In cold weather, warm the paste slightly in the oven.

If a crust has formed, remove before use.

Protect coloured sugarpaste from strong light.

Sugarpaste can be flavoured with a drop or two of flavouring to counteract sweetness.

Roll out sugarpaste on an icing sugar dusted surface.

The drying time for sugarpaste varies with the weather and conditions in the kitchen. 24 hours is an approximate time. Sugarpaste should be crimped before it dries.

When crimping, hold the crimper at right angles to the cake and push gently into the paste before squeezing the crimper. Release the pressure and remove carefully.

FIXING

Butter icing or jam should be used to join sponge cakes.

Use cooled boiled water or clear liquor when fixing sugarpaste to sugarpaste.

Use royal icing or cooled boiled water when fixing sugarpaste figures to sugarpaste.

Fix ribbons with small dots or fine lines of royal icing.

STIPPLING

Use a palette knife to stipple large areas or a sponge for small, fine areas.

FRILL

Frill sugarpaste by rolling the pointed end of a cocktail stick or paintbrush along the edge a little at a time.

PORTIONS

A 20.5cm (8in) round sponge will provide approximately 16 portions.

FREEZING

Batch baked swiss rolls and sponges can be frozen for up to six months. Swiss rolls can be rolled up before freezing and stored unfilled.

HAPPY MONSTER

INGREDIENTS

20.5cm round sponge (8in)
2 required
1.25k sugarpaste (2½lb)
115g royal icing (4oz)
Assorted food colours

EQUIPMENT and DECORATIONS

30.5cm oval cake board (12cm)
Piping tubes No.1 and 42
Candle and holder
Board edge ribbon

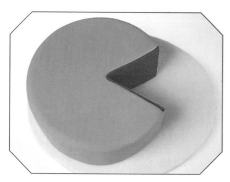

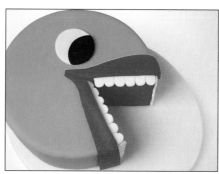

1 Cut out a wedge from the round sponge and cover the main piece with sugarpaste. Cover the oval board with sugarpaste and then place the cake as shown.

2 Cut out and fix sugarpaste teeth, lips and eye.

3 Cover the wedge with sugarpaste and decorate as required. Pipe inscription of choice (No.1).

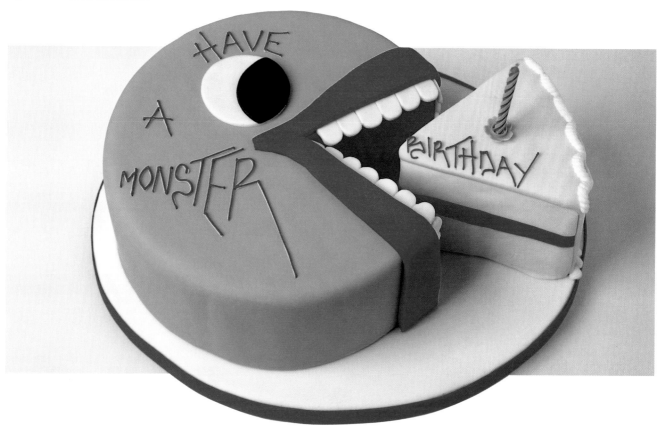

DOLLS HOUSE

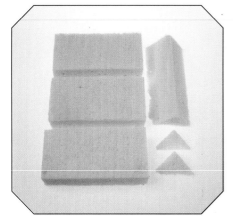

1 Using the template as a guide, cut the sponges in half and then angle one of the pieces into a roof shape.

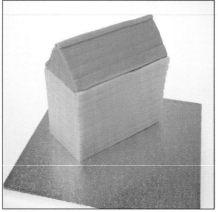

2 Stack the pieces together, layer with filling and cover with sugarpaste. Make lines, using a ruler.

3 Fix additional roof pieces. Pipe shells as shown (No.6).

20.5cm square sponge (8in)
  2 required
680g sugarpaste (1½lb)
225g royal icing (8oz)
Assorted food colours

25.5cm square cake
  board (10in)
Fine sponge
Ruler
Paintbrush
Piping tube No.6

Butterfly
Birthday motto
Flowers
Doll
Board edge ribbon

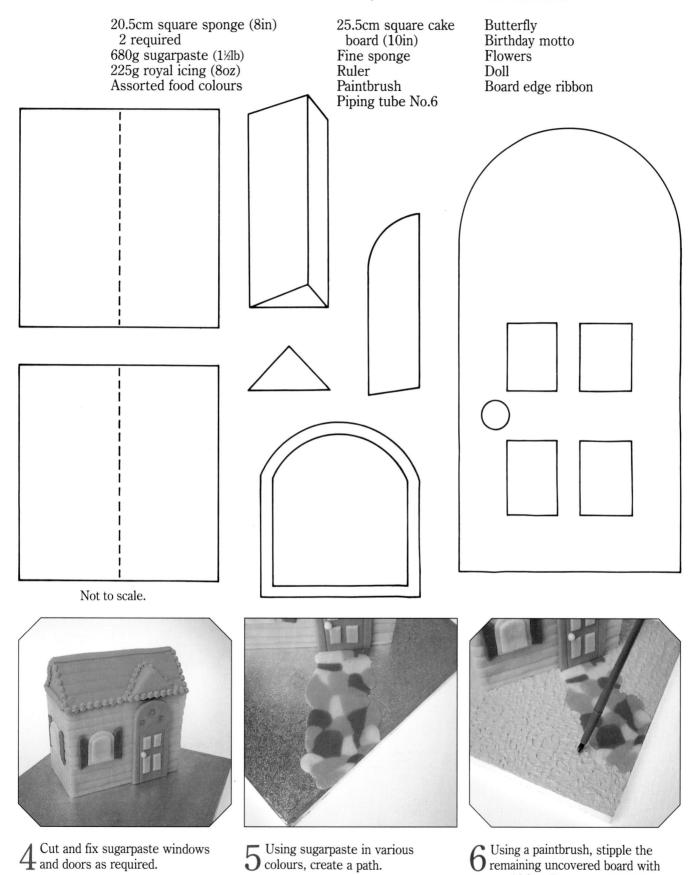

Not to scale.

4 Cut and fix sugarpaste windows and doors as required.

5 Using sugarpaste in various colours, create a path.

6 Using a paintbrush, stipple the remaining uncovered board with royal icing. Decorate with flowers, motto and doll.

SCHOOL PACK

1 Cut sponges to form basic shape of a carrying case, flask and box. Coat in butter icing and place in refrigerator to chill.

2 Cover each item with sugarpaste, indenting the lines with a ruler or straight edge.

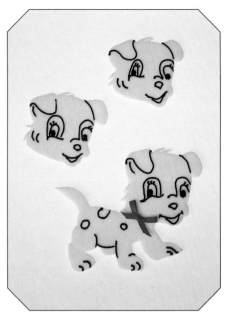

3 Using the template as a guide, cut out sugarpaste puppy and heads. Pipe the lines with royal icing (No.1). Leave to dry.

4 Fix the puppy to the carrying case then make and fix a sugarpaste handle and lock.

5 Fix a head to the top of the box.

6 Fix the last head to the flask, then make and fix a sugarpaste handle. Place all the cakes onto a sugarpaste covered board.

INGREDIENTS

20.5cm square sponge (8in)
 2 required
900g sugarpaste (2lb)
115g royal icing (4oz)
Assorted food colours

EQUIPMENT and DECORATIONS

28cm square cake board
 (11in)
Decorative board covering
Cake card
Ruler
Piping tube No.1
Ribbon bow
Board edge ribbon

STEREO

INGREDIENTS

15 x 10cm sponge cake
  (6 x 4in) 2 required
900g sugarpaste (2lb)
115g royal icing (4oz)
Assorted food colours

EQUIPMENT and DECORATIONS

23cm square cake board (9in)
Decorative board covering
Cake card
Piping tube No.1

1 Layer and fix the sponges together. Place upright and cover with sugarpaste. Stand on cake card then fix to the cake board. Cut and fix a piece of sugarpaste to the front.

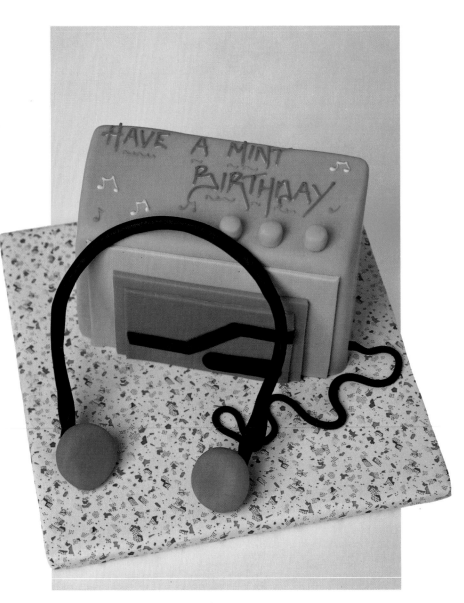

2 Cut out and fix various shapes of sugarpaste to the front and top as shown.

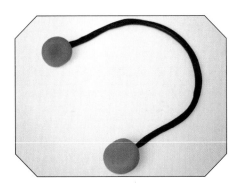

3 Make a set of head phones using sugarpaste. Fix to the personal stereo with a sugarpaste wire. Pipe inscription and music notes with royal icing (No.1).

HOPPIE

INGREDIENTS

20.5cm round sponge (8in)
  2 required
1.25k sugarpaste (2½lb)
115g royal icing (4oz)
Assorted food colours

EQUIPMENT and DECORATIONS

28cm round cake board (11in)
Crimper
2 drinking straws
Piping tube No.2
Party blower
Board edge ribbon

1 Cover the cake and board separately with different coloured sugarpaste. Then half mix the two colours together, roll out, fix to the cake-base and crimp.

2 Cut out and fix sugarpaste eyes.

3 Cut out and fix sugarpaste pupils and mouth. Pipe dots for nose and fix plastic straws for antennae. Fix party blower. Then pipe inscription of choice with royal icing (No.2).

IGUANODON

1 Cover the cake with mottled sugarpaste.

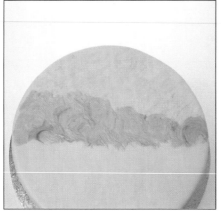

2 Stipple royal icing for the sky then use a palette knife to create the hills.

3 Brush on icing for the rocks and ground. Continue the ground around the cake-side.

23cm round sponge (9in)
 2 required
1.5k sugarpaste (3lb)
225g royal icing (8oz)
Assorted food colours

28cm round cake board (11in)
Piping tube No.1
Palette knife
Paintbrush
Plastic motto

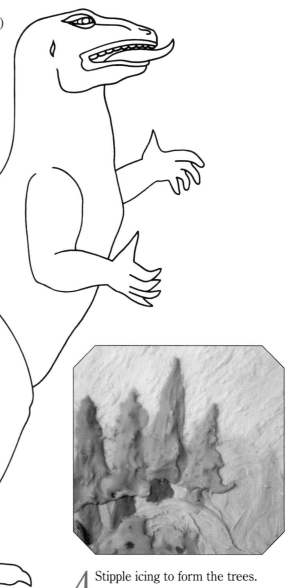

4 Stipple icing to form the trees.

5 Using the template as a guide, cut out the Iguanodon from sugarpaste. Smooth the sides then indent with the end of a paintbrush to form the grooves.

6 Brush the Iguanodon with colouring then complete the face with royal icing.

7 Pipe desert plants around the cake-side then make and fix sugarpaste rocks.

MAGIC HAT

INGREDIENTS

15cm round sponge (6in)
 4 required
1.5k sugarpaste (3lb)
115g royal icing (4oz)
Black and red food colours
Edible silver colour
Pink dusting powder

EQUIPMENT and DECORATIONS

38cm round cake board (15in)
20.5cm cake card (8in)
Decorative board covering
Piping tube No.1
Board edge ribbon

1 Layer the sponges together and cut out a hole in the top sponge. Cover with sugarpaste. Cut a hole out of the cake card, cover both sides with sugarpaste and fix to the sponge top.

2 Make and fix a pair of rabbit ears from sugarpaste. Colour with dusting powder.

3 Make and fix a sugarpaste card, wand and silk scarf. Pipe inscription of choice on the card with royal icing (No.1).

OCTOPUS

INGREDIENTS

25.5cm hexagonal sponge
(10in) 2 required
Sponge baked in a 600ml
pudding basin (1pt)

2k sugarpaste (4lb)
225g royal icing (8oz)
60g Demerara sugar (2oz)
Assorted food colours

EQUIPMENT and DECORATIONS

30.5cm hexagonal
cake board (12in)
Fine sponge
Piping tube No.1
Board edge ribbon

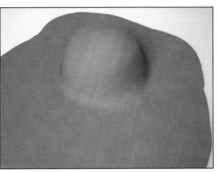

1 Fix the sponge to the cake board.
Cover with sugarpaste. Stipple the
board with royal icing then sprinkle
with demerara sugar. Cut and fix
sugarpaste seaweed.

2 Cover the pudding shaped sponge
with a large piece of sugarpaste.
Cut the tentacles to form the
octopus.

3 Fix the octopus to the cake-top.
Cut and fix sugarpaste eyes and
suckers. Make and decorate the
hat. Pipe name (No.1).

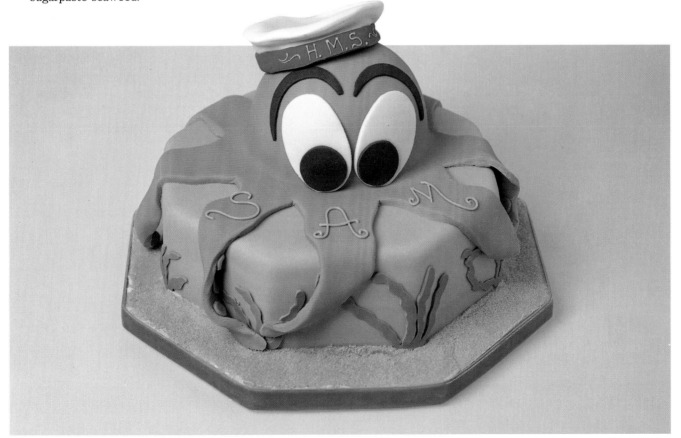

FLOWER FAIRY

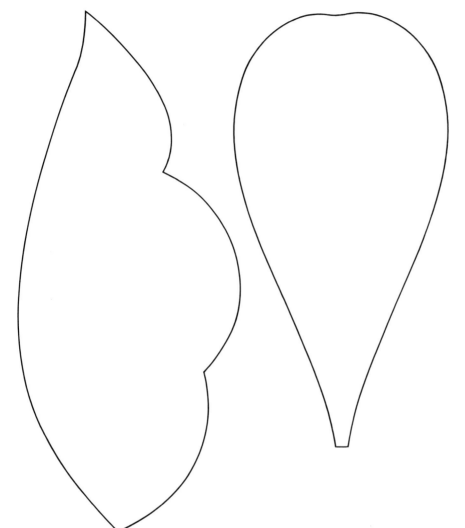

1 Coat the sponge with butter icing. Fix to the cake board. Make and fix mottled sugarpaste frills, in layers, from the base to the top. Stipple the board with royal icing.

2 Cut out, crimp and fix sugarpaste petal shapes as shown.

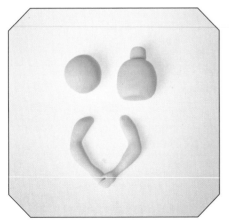

3 Mould sugarpaste head and arms as shown.

4 Make and fix a sugarpaste body to the cake-top, then head and arms. Cut out and fix sugarpaste petals and hat. Pipe flower motifs on skirt (No.1).

5 Using the templates as a guide cut out rice paper wings. Decorate with dusting powder then fix to the back with a little water. Fix flowers to the hands and cake board.

Sponge baked in a 15cm
  bell shaped tin (6in)
900g sugarpaste (2lb)
225g royal icing (8oz)
Assorted food colours

25.5cm petal shaped cake
  board (10in)
Piping tube No.1
Pink dusting powder
Rice paper
Fine paint brush

Palette knife
Crimper
Cocktail stick
Assorted blossoms
Board edge ribbon

CAMERA

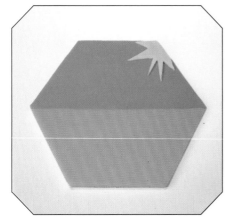

1 Cover the cake board with sugarpaste to form horizon and the sun.

2 Coat a sponge and swiss roll with butter icing. Leave in refrigerator for 1 hour to harden.

3 Cover the sponges with sugarpaste, join together on the covered cake board to form the camera.

INGREDIENTS

Half a swiss roll
18 x 10cm sponge (7 x 4in)
  2 required
900g sugar paste (2lb)
115g royal icing (4oz)
Assorted food colours

EQUIPMENT and DECORATIONS

28cm hexagonal cake
  board (11in)
Piping tube No.2
Photograph
Silver paper
Board edge ribbon

4 Cut out and fix various sugarpaste shapes for the camera parts. Then mould and fix a strap.

5 Cut out and fix a photograph (backed with silver paper) then fix additional sugarpaste parts as shown.

6 Pipe inscription of choice (No.2). Fix ribbon around the cake board.

OUR TWINS

INGREDIENTS

20.5 square sponge (8in)
 2 required
900g sugarpaste (2lb)
225g royal icing (8oz)
Assorted dusting powders
Assorted food colours

EQUIPMENT and DECORATIONS

28cm square cake board (11in)
Blossom cutters
Fine paint brush
Piping tubes No.1, 2 and 7
Dragees
Board edge ribbon

1 Cover the cake and board with sugarpaste. Using the templates as a guide, cut out sugarpaste teddy bears. Leave until dry.

Increase the templates according to the size of the cake being decorated.

2 Cut out and decorate sugarpaste party hats and balloons.

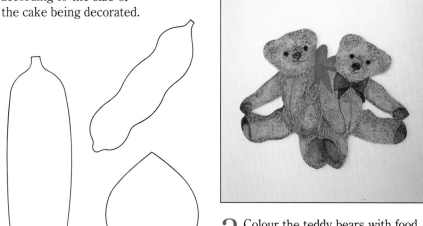

3 Colour the teddy bears with food colours and dusting powders, as shown.

4 When dry, fix the teddy bears to the cake-top. Pipe grass with royal icing (No.1). Make and fix sugarpaste flowers.

5 Pipe rosettes around the cake-base (No.7) then decorate with dragees. Fix the balloons and hats to the cake-sides.

6 Pipe the lines shown around the cake-top edge (No.2). Pipe inscription of choice (No.1). Make and fix sugarpaste flowers around the cake board.

WRESTLING

1 Cover the cake-top and board with sugarpaste. Then cover the sides, marking with a ruler, to form curtain effect.

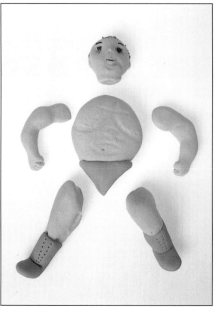

2 Mould the various parts of the first wrestler with sugarpaste, as shown.

3 Make the feet of second wrestler and fix all the parts together on the cake-top.

4 Make and fix the body.

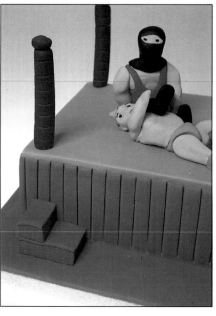

5 Insert a piece of dowling into each corner and cover with sugarpaste. Make and fix steps.

6 Fix ribbons around the corner posts. Pipe inscription of choice with royal icing (No.1).

20.5 square sponge (8in)
  2 required
1.25k sugarpaste (2½lb)
225g modelling paste (8oz)
115g royal icing (4oz)
Assorted food colours

28cm square cake board (11in)
Dowling
Ruler
Piping tube No.1
Narrow ribbons
Board edge ribbon

MOONBEAM

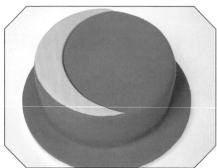

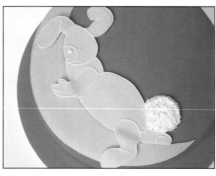

1 Cover the cake and board with sugarpaste. Using the template as a guide, cut and fix sugarpaste moon.

2 Cut out and fix the sugarpaste rabbit. Pipe the lines and tail with royal icing (No.1).

3 Cut out and fix sugarpaste stars and shooting star. Pipe inscription of choice (No.1).

INGREDIENTS

20.5 round sponge (8in)
 2 required
900g sugarpaste (2lb)
115g royal icing (4oz)
Assorted food colours

EQUIPMENT and DECORATIONS

28cm round cake board (11in)
Star shaped cutters
Piping tube No.1
Board edge ribbon

PIRATE BOAT

INGREDIENTS

Sponge baked in a 900g
  loaf tin (2lb)
680g sugarpaste (1½lb)
340g royal icing (12oz)
Liquorice sticks
Spaghetti strands
Rice paper
Fish sweets
Assorted food colours

EQUIPMENT and DECORATIONS

35.5 x 25.5cm cake board
  (14 x 10in)
Ruler
Fine paint brush
Black food pen
Piping tube No.1
Cake card
Board edge ribbon

1 Layer, then cut the sponges into a boat shape. Cover with sugarpaste and mark with a ruler and paint brush to form nailed planks.

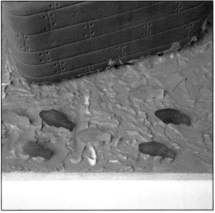

2 Fix the cake to the board. Stipple royal icing over the board to form sea, then fix the fish.

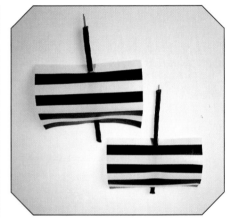

3 Mark stripes onto rice paper sails. Push a spaghetti strand down the middle of each liquorice stick then insert the sails.

4 Insert masts into deck. Make and fix a flag. Fix liquorice gunwale around the cake-top and then an anchor as shown.

5 Make and decorate a variety of sugarpaste pirates.

6 Make and fix a sugarpaste plank. Then fix the pirates as required. Make and decorate a sugarpaste plaque. Pipe inscription of choice and name the boat (No.1).

JUNIOR SCRABBLE

INGREDIENTS

25.5cm square sponge (10in)
  2 required
1.75k sugarpaste (3½lb)
225g royal icing (8oz)
Assorted food colours

EQUIPMENT and DECORATIONS

33cm square cake board (13in)
Piping tubes No.2 and 44
Assorted novelty cutters
Assorted small toys
Board edge ribbon

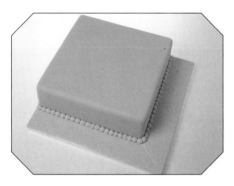

1 Cover the cake with sugarpaste. Fix to one corner of the board then cover the board with sugarpaste. Pipe shells around the front two edges of the cake-base with royal icing (No.44).

2 Cut out and fix sugarpaste squares then pipe each letter required (No.2). Make extra for the cake board.

3 Fix sugarpaste cut outs around the cake-sides. Place the extra squares onto the cake board. Cut out and place sugarpaste markers. Decorate the cake-top with small toys.

DOGGY PADDLE

INGREDIENTS

20.5cm round sponge (8in)
  2 required
900g sugarpaste (2lb)
225g royal icing (8oz)
Assorted food colours

EQUIPMENT and DECORATIONS

25.5cm round cake
  board (10in)
Piping tubes No.1 and 2
Fine sponge

Ruler
Palette knife
Sugarpaste flowers
Board edge ribbon

1 Layer, then cover the sponge with sugarpaste around the side. Mark to form bricks. Fix a thin layer of sugarpaste over the top. Fix a rim. Stipple the board with royal icing.

2 Mould the pieces in sequence above, using sugarpaste, to make a dog. Make a selection of dogs in various positions on swimming pool items.

3 Spread royal icing over the top, fix the sugarpaste items, then swirl the icing to form ripples. Pipe ladder and inscription (No.2 and 1). Decorate with sugarpaste flowers.

SPACE SHUTTLE

INGREDIENTS

30.5cm round sponge (12in)
  2 required
1 large swiss roll
450g butter icing (1lb)

450g sugarpaste (1lb)
60g demerara sugar (2oz)
Assorted food colours

EQUIPMENT and DECORATIONS

40.5 x 30.5cm cake board (16 x 12in)
Piping tube No.1
Palette knife
Board edge ribbon

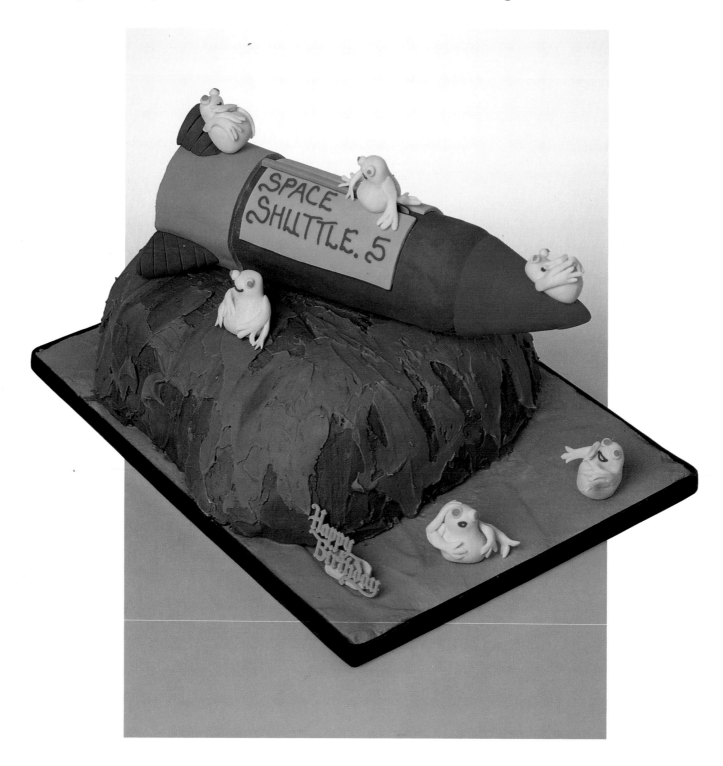

1 Layer, then cut the round sponges to an irregular shape. Coat roughly with grey coloured butter icing.

2 Fix onto the cake board. Stipple royal icing onto the remaining board surface and sprinkle with demerara sugar. Spread green butter icing over cake, as shown.

3 Shape the swiss roll to form the rocket and cover with sugarpaste.

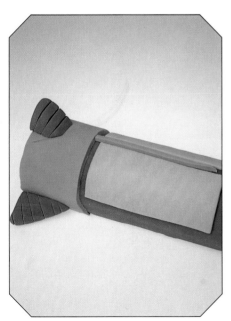

4 Make and fix sugarpaste pieces to the rocket, as shown.

5 Make and decorate sugarpaste moon beams with royal icing (No.1).

6 Fix the rocket and moon beams to the cake as required. Pipe inscription (No.1).

PIZZA

INGREDIENTS

23cm round sponge (9in)
680g sugarpaste (1½lb)
225g royal icing (8oz)
Assorted food colours

EQUIPMENT and DECORATIONS

25.5cm round cake board (10in)
Fine paint brush
Palette knife
Drinking straw
Board edge ribbon

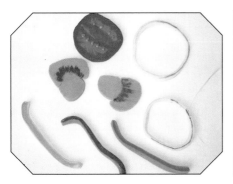  

1 Cover the sponge and board with sugarpaste. Make and colour a wide selection of sugarpaste vegetables.

2 Spread royal icing over the cake-top, using a palette knife.

3 Immediately fix the vegetables onto the royal icing. Push some sugarpaste through a grater to form cheese pieces. Make and decorate a flag with inscription of choice.

PARTY CAN

INGREDIENTS

20.5 square sponge (8in)
  2 required
Swiss roll
900g sugarpaste (2lb)
Assorted food colours

EQUIPMENT and DECORATIONS

28cm square cake board (11in)
Cake card
Decorative board covering
Ribbon
Piping tubes No.2 and 3
Round cutter

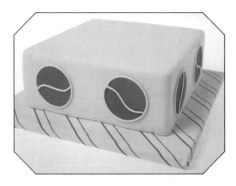

1 Cover board with decorative paper. Cover cake with sugarpaste. Place on cake card, fix to the board. Cut out circles and fill with coloured sugarpaste. Pipe lines with royal icing (No.3).

2 Cover a swiss roll, cut to the shape of half a can, with sugarpaste. Fix to cake top. Fix ribbon around cake-base.

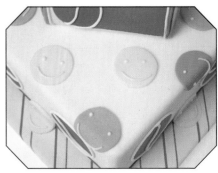

3 Cut out and fix sugarpaste circles, pipe the faces (No.2). Cut and place sugarpaste streamers as shown.

GRAND PIANO

INGREDIENTS

20.5cm round sponge (8in)
  2 required
900g sugarpaste (2lb)
115g royal icing (4oz)
Assorted food colours

EQUIPMENT and DECORATIONS

30.5cm oval cake board (12in)
Decorative board covering
20.5cm round cake card (8in)
  2 required
Piping tubes No.1 and 42
Cake pillars or plastic dowel
  3 required
Small palette knife
Artificial blossoms
Board edge ribbon

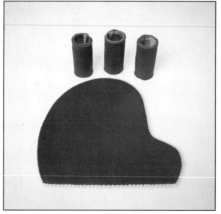

1 Using the template as a guide, cut out the piano shape from the sponge and a cake card, then cover with sugarpaste.

2 Using the template as a guide, cut out a thin cake card and cover with sugarpaste, for the lid. Cover 3 pieces of plastic dowel or pillars, with sugarpaste for the legs.

3 Cut and fix sugarpaste keys and music sheet. Fix the lid then pipe shells with royal icing, around the edge (No.42).

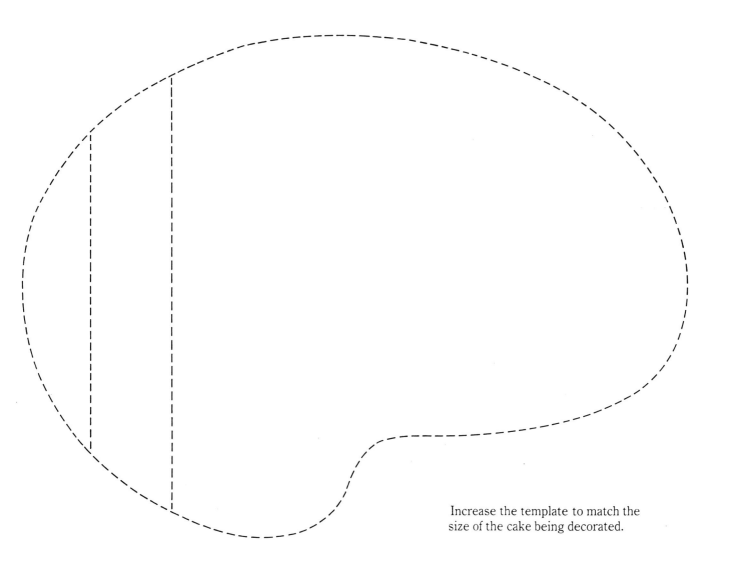

Increase the template to match the size of the cake being decorated.

4 Make a piano stool with sponge off cuts and fluted sugarpaste. Stand on small piece of cake card.

5 Make a sugarpaste rug as shown. Place on small piece of cake card.

6 Make a spotty dog in the position shown. Assemble on covered board. Pipe and decorate inscription of choice (No.1).

TURTLE

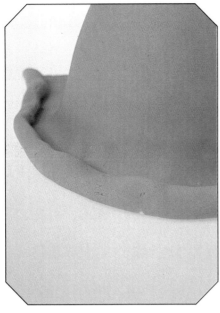

INGREDIENTS

Sponge baked in a 1.2Lt
  pudding basin (2pt)
900g sugarpaste (2lb)
225g royal icing (8oz)
Assorted food colours

EQUIPMENT and DECORATIONS

25.5cm round cake board (10in)
Hexagonal cake pillar
Palette knife
Fine sponge
Board edge ribbon

1 Roll out the sugarpaste to more than cover the sponge. Place over the sponge and roll up the excess around the base.

2 Continue rolling up the edge to form bridges for the feet, head and tail. Press the end of a cake pillar over the top to form the pattern shown.

3 Make the head from sugarpaste.

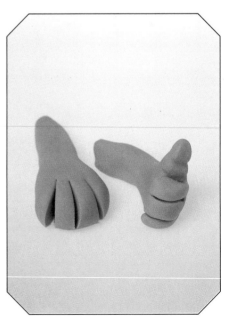

4 Mould and cut the sugarpaste hands.

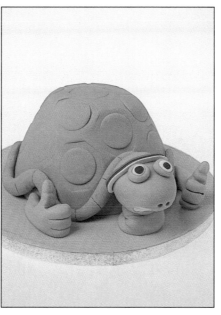

5 Mould and fix sugarpaste parts to form two trainers.

6 Place the sponge onto the board then stipple with royal icing to form grass effect. Fix the head and hands.

7 Fix the feet and trainers, make and fix a tail.

TEDDY'S PARTY

INGREDIENTS

15cm round sponge (6in)
  4 required
1.25k sugarpaste (2½lb)
340g royal icing (12oz)
Dusting powders
Assorted food colours

EQUIPMENT and DECORATIONS

30.5cm petal shaped cake
  board (12in)
Rice paper
Fine paint brush
Piping tube No.2
Board edge ribbon

1 Layer the sponges together. Then cover with mottled sugarpaste and mark with a fork to form the bark. Fix to the board and stipple with royal icing.

2 Cut out and decorate a selection of sugarpaste bears.

3 Make and decorate a selection of mushrooms, hive, bees and flowers with sugarpaste, rice paper and royal icing.

4 When dry, fix a bear to the cake-side. Make and fix a honey pot. Pipe honey with royal icing as shown.

5 Fix bears around the cake-base. Decorate the cake board with mushrooms and flowers.

6 Fix hive and bees to the cake-top as required. Pipe inscription of choice (No.2).

Increase the templates according to the size of the cake being decorated.

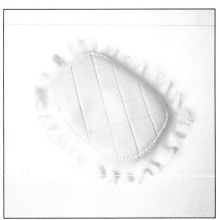

1 Cover the board with decorative paper. Cut and fix sugarpaste around cake-side. Stand on cake card. Cut and fix sugarpaste onto the cake-top then press edge with fluted modelling tool.

2 Make a sugarpaste pillow. Pipe the edge with royal icing (No.1).

3 Fix the pillow to the cake-top. Make and fix a sugarpaste head and long cone shape for the body.

20.5 x 15cm sponge cake
  (8 x 6in) 2 required
680g modelling paste (1½lb)
1.5k sugarpaste (3lb)
225g royal icing (8oz)
Assorted dusting powders
Assorted food colours

40.5 x 35.5cm cake board (16 x 14in)
Decorative board covering
Cake card
Paintbrush
Piping tubes No.1 and 2

Edible pens
Palette knife
Modelling tool

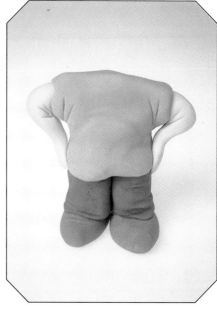

4 Cut and fix a sugarpaste bed cover.

5 **To make a friend:** roll out sugarpaste for legs, then mould shoes as shown.

6 Fix the legs into the shoes and push down to form creases. Mould and fix body and arms.

7 Mould and fix the face. Fix the nose. Paint the eyes and eyebrows with edible pens.

8 Brush the cheeks with dusting powder. Pipe the beard with royal icing (No.2). Make and fix a hat.

9 Picture shows the completed friend. Make six further friends as shown overleaf.

10 Repeat steps 5 to 8 to make a friend in the character shown.

11 Repeat steps 5 to 8 to make a friend in the character shown.

12 Repeat steps 5 to 8 to make a friend in the character shown.

13 Repeat steps 5 to 8 to make a friend in the character shown.

14 Repeat steps 5 to 8 to make a friend in the character shown.

15 Repeat steps 5 to 8 to make a friend in the character shown. Fix the friends as required.

BOUNCING HIPPO'S

INGREDIENTS

20.5cm square sponge (8in)
  2 required
1.25k sugarpaste (2½lb)
115g royal icing (4oz)
Assorted food colours

EQUIPMENT and DECORATIONS

30.5cm square cake board (12in)
Fork
Piping tubes No.1 and 43
Board edge ribbon

 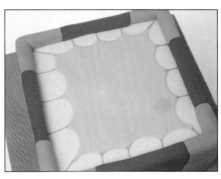 

1 Cover cake-top with sugarpaste. Mould and fix a sugarpaste roll around the edge. Cover the sides and edge with sugarpaste. Cover the board with sugarpaste and mark to form grass effect.

2 Cut out and fix sugarpaste canvas sheet top. Pipe the lines with royal icing (No.1).

3 Mould and decorate sugarpaste hippopotami. Fix to the cake-top. Pipe barrel scrolls around the cake-base (No.43). Pipe message on the cake board (No.1).

FIRE ENGINE

INGREDIENTS

25.5cm square sponge cake
  (10in) 2 required
1.5k sugarpaste (3lb)
115g modelling paste (4oz)
115g royal icing (4oz)
Liquorice pin wheels
Assorted food colours

EQUIPMENT and DECORATIONS

38 x 30.5cm cake board
  (15 x 12in)
Coarse mesh
Piping tubes No.3 and 4
Board edge ribbon

1 Cover the board with sugarpaste and mark with coarse mesh, to form road. Cut out and fix sugarpaste road lines. Cut one sponge in half, trim the sides and cover with sugarpaste, for the base.

2 Cut and layer the remaining sponges. Cover with sugarpaste and fix to the base.

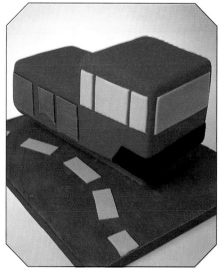

3 Cut and fix sugarpaste windows and doors, as shown.

4 Make and fix sugarpaste lights, wheels and trimmings.

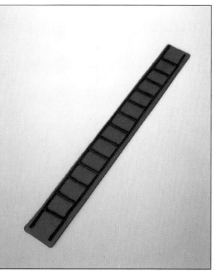

5 Cut out a strip of modelling paste for the ladder. Pipe royal icing lines to form the runners (No.4). Leave until dry then fix to the engine.

6 Partly unroll a liquorice wheel and fix as shown. Pipe message of choice (No.3).

HELTER SKELTER

INGREDIENTS

10cm round sponge cake (4in)
  4 required
1.5k sugarpaste (3lb)
115g royal icing (4oz)
Assorted food colours

EQUIPMENT and DECORATIONS

25.5cm round cake board (10in)
Candles and holders
Birthday motto
Board edge ribbon

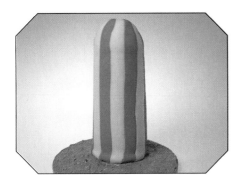

1 Layer and stack the sponges together, trimming the top to dome shape. Cover with strips of sugarpaste. Stipple the board with royal icing then fix the sponge in the position shown.

2 Cut out and fix a sugarpaste slide. Leave to dry for 1 hour.

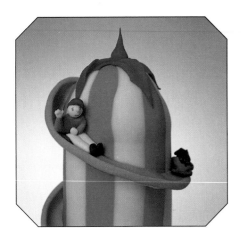

3 Decorate the top with sugarpaste leaves and pinnacle. Make and fix a variety of sugarpaste figures. Fix candles and holders to the board.

FORT MYER

INGREDIENTS

25.5cm square sponge (10in)
20.5cm square sponge (8in)
  2 required
15cm square sponge (6in)
  2 required
10cm square sponge (4in)
  2 required
2k sugarpaste (4lb)
340g royal icing (12oz)
Black, green and blue food
  colours

EQUIPMENT and DECORATIONS

40.5cm round cake board (16in)
Ruler
Plastic figures
Flag
Candles and holders
Palette knife
Board edge ribbon

1 Layer matching sized sponges, cover with sugarpaste and mark sides with ruler to form stones.

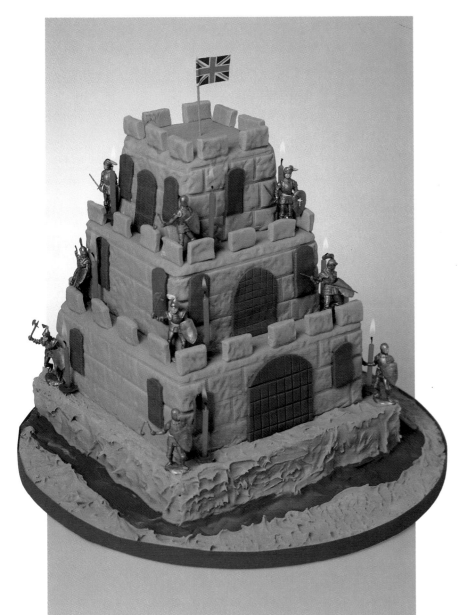

2 Cut out and fix sugarpaste stones, windows and doors.

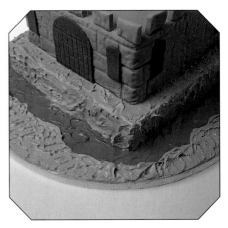

3 Layer and stack the sponges together. Stipple the base sponge and around the board with royal icing, as shown. Fix candles, flag and figures as required.

TOADSTOOL

INGREDIENTS

20.5cm round sponge (8in)
 2 required
1.5k sugarpaste (3lb)
225g royal icing (8oz)
Assorted food colours

EQUIPMENT and DECORATIONS

30.5cm round cake board (12in)
Coarse wire sieve
Fine sponge
Piping tube No.1

Blossom cutter
Plastic gnomes
Board edge ribbon

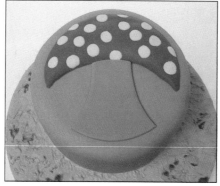

1 Cover the cake with sugarpaste and place it onto the cake board in the position shown. Stipple the board with royal icing to form the ground.

2 Using the template as a guide, cut out and fix a sugarpaste toadstool.

3 Cut out and fix the door, windows and chimney.

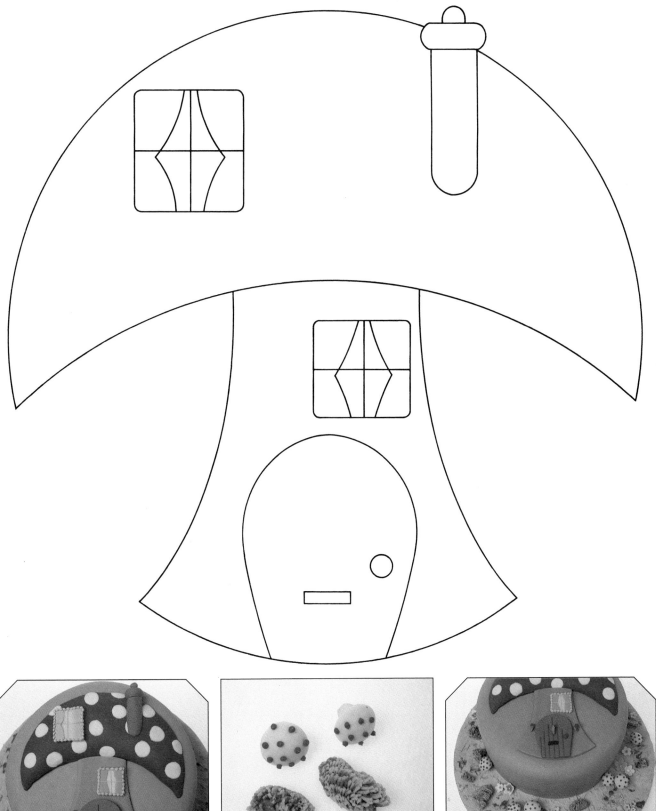

4 Decorate the various pieces with royal icing, as shown.

5 Make a selection of toadstools, sugarpaste pushed through a sieve to form brushes, together with cut out flowers.

6 Fix to the board then decorate with plastic gnomes. Pipe inscription of choice on the cake-top (No.1) then decorate with flowers.

HEAVY METAL

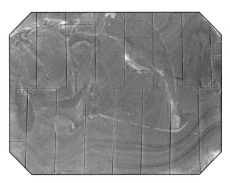

INGREDIENTS

20.5cm square sponge (8in)
  2 required
1.5k sugarpaste (3lb)
225g royal icing (8oz)
Assorted food colours

EQUIPMENT and DECORATIONS

28cm square cake board (11in)
Piping tube No.1
Fine sponge
Marker
Palette knife
Board edge ribbon

1 Cover the top of the cake with mottled sugarpaste. Mark to create floorboard effect.

2 Roll out sugarpaste, gather and fix to the cake sides to form a curtain. Stipple the board with royal icing.

3 Make a sugarpaste drummer, sitting on a stool, and decorate with royal icing.

4 Make and decorate a guitarist, as shown.

5 Make and decorate a second guitarist.

6 Make and decorate a lead singer.

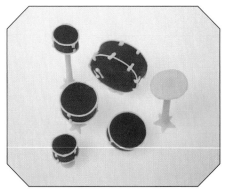

7 Make and decorate a drum set. Fix all pieces to the cake-top then pipe inscription (No.1).

LADYBIRD

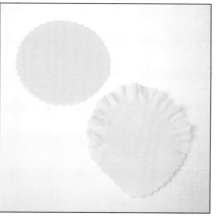

1 Layer, then cover the sponges with sugarpaste, place onto the cake board then stipple royal icing over the board.

2 Cut out sugarpaste disc the same diameter as the petal leaves, shape and frill by rolling a cocktail stick backwards and forwards along the edge a little at a time.

3 Fix petals to cake-top, overlapping as shown. Mould and fix a sugarpaste dome to form the flower centre, using a coarse sieve to create the fine criss cross pattern.

25.5cm petal shaped sponge
  (10in) 2 required
1.75k sugarpaste (3½lb)
225g royal icing (8oz)
Assorted food colours

33cm round cake board (13in)
Coarse sieve
Piping tubes No.1 and 2
Palette knife
Cocktail stick
Board edge ribbon

4 Cut, frill and fix sugarpaste around the cake-base. Make a sugarpaste ladybird.

5 Fix the ladybird to the cake-top then pipe the legs (No.1). 2 ladybirds required.

6 Pipe shells around the cake-base (No.2). Make and fix tiny sugarpaste ladybirds around the cake-side. Pipe the legs (No.1). Pipe inscription as required (No.1).

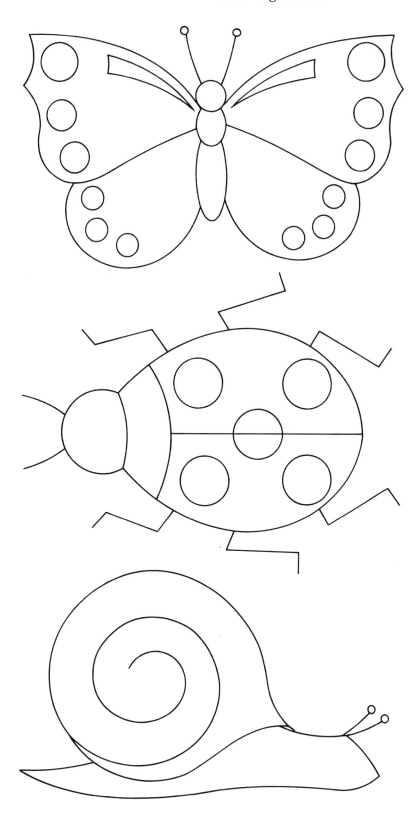

1 Cover board with paper. Slice sponge at an angle, turn top over then cover with sugarpaste. Stand on cake card. Mark edges to form pages. Cut and fix sugarpaste around the cake-base as shown.

2 Using the template as a guide, draw the picture and words onto rice paper, with food approved pens.

3 Repeat step 2 for the second page, as shown.

30.5 x 15cm sponge (12 x 6in)
  2 required
1.25k sugarpaste (2½lb)
225g royal icing (8oz)
Assorted dusting powders
Assorted food colours

35.5 x 25.5cm cake
  board (14 x 10in)
Decorative board
  covering
Cake card
Rice paper

Food approved pens
Palette knife
Fine paint brush
Piping tubes No.1 and 2

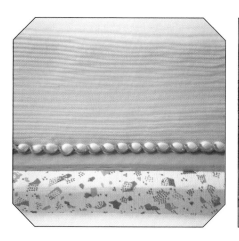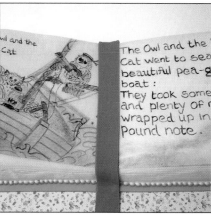

4 Pipe shells (No.2) with royal icing around the cake-base. Pipe a line over the shells (No.1).

5 Fix the pages to the cake-top, using royal icing. Then cut and fix a sugarpaste bookmark.

6 Cut and fix sugarpaste music notes around the board.

25.5 round sponge (10in)
2 required
1.5k sugarpaste (3lb)
450g royal icing (1lb)
Assorted food colours

33cm round cake board (13in)
Paint brush
Piping tube No.1
Palette knife
Board edge ribbon

1 Cut the sides of the cake to an irregular pattern. Cover with sugarpaste, place onto the board then stipple the board with royal icing to create the sea.

2 Using the templates as a guide, cut out penguins from sugarpaste as required. Leave to dry for 24 hours. Then colour and fix the large penguin to the cake-top.

3 Colour and fix the small penguins as shown. Pipe inscription with royal icing (No.1).

71

The cake's message reads: WELL DONE DUNCAN

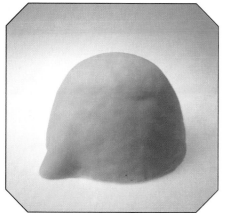

1 Shape a sugarpaste nose onto the side of the sponge, then cover with sugarpaste.

INGREDIENTS

Sponge baked in a 1.2Lt
  pudding basin (2pt)
680g sugarpaste (1½lb)
225g royal icing (8oz)
Assorted food colours

EQUIPMENT and DECORATIONS

30.5 x 25.5 cake board (12 x 10in)
Piping tube No.1
Palette knife
Board edge ribbon

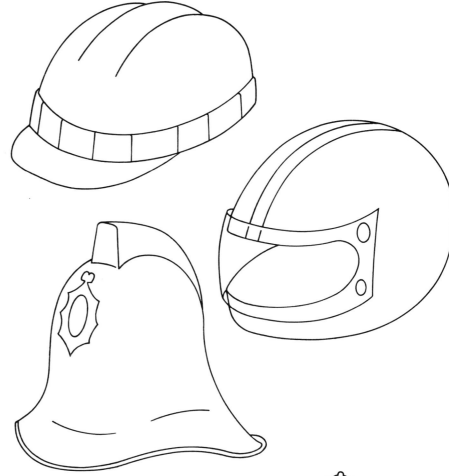

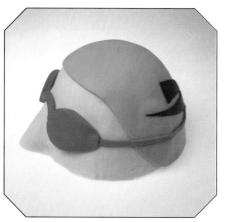

2 Cut out and fix a sugarpaste hat.

3 Cut out and fix sugarpaste hat designs and goggles.

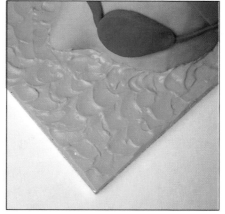

4 Place the cake onto the cake board and spread royal icing to create water effect. Make and decorate a sugarpaste plaque.

NURSE

INGREDIENTS

20.5cm round sponge (8in)
  2 required
13cm round sponge (5in)
  2 required
1.5k sugarpaste (3lb)
115g royal icing (4oz)
Assorted food colours

EQUIPMENT and DECORATIONS

35.5cm oval cake board (14in)
Piping tubes No.1 and 2
Paint brush
Ribbon bow
Cocktail stick
Board edge ribbon

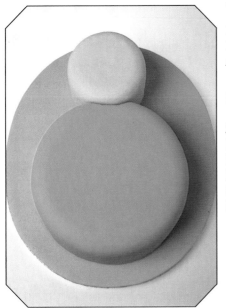

1 Cover the sponges and cake board with sugarpaste, as shown.

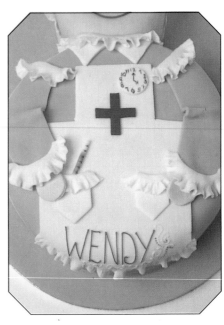

2 Cut out, frill and fix sugarpaste apron and collar.

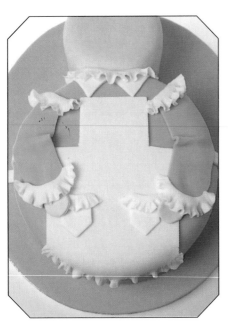

3 Cut and fix sugarpaste arms, hands and apron strings.

Pipe face and hair with royal icing (No.2).

5 Decorate the apron with a sugarpaste watch and thermometer. Pipe inscription (No.1).

PUSSY CAT

INGREDIENTS

20.5cm round sponge (8in)
 2 required
900g sugarpaste (2lb)
225g royal icing (8oz)
Assorted food colours

EQUIPMENT and DECORATIONS

30.5cm oval cake board (12in)
Fine sponge
Piping tubes No.1 and 2
Spaghetti strands
Ribbon bow
Palette knife
Board edge ribbon

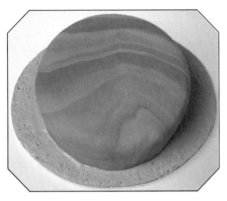

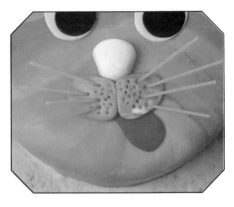

1 Layer and cover the sponges with mottled sugarpaste. Place onto the cake board and then stipple the board with royal icing.

2 Cut and fix sugarpaste ears and eyes.

3 Cut and fix sugarpaste nose, mouth and tongue. Use spaghetti for whiskers. Pipe inscription of choice on the cake board (No.1).

BOUNCING CASTLE

INGREDIENTS

20.5cm square sponge (8in)
 2 required
Mini swiss roll 4 required
1.5k sugarpaste (3lb)
225g royal icing (8oz)
Assorted food colours

EQUIPMENT and DECORATIONS

30.5cm square cake board (12in)
Piping tube No.43
Happy birthday ribbon
4 Union Jack flags
Novelty cake candle
Artificial or sugarpaste blossoms
Palette knife
Board edge ribbon

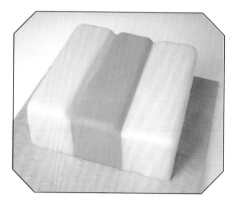

1 Cut two thin wedges from the cake-top then cover with sugarpaste. Then stipple the board with royal icing.

2 Cover the swiss rolls with sugarpaste to form turrets. Cut the bases at a slight angle.

3 Fix the turrets to the cake-top. Cut and fix sugarpaste edge. Make and fix sugarpaste figures. Decorate the cake board with flowers.

PARTY TRAIN

INGREDIENTS

30.5 x 20.5cm sponge cake
  (12 x 8in) 2 required
1.75k sugarpaste (3½lb)
225g royal icing (8oz)
Assorted food colours

EQUIPMENT and DECORATIONS

30.5 x 25.5cm cake board
  (14 x 10in)
Piping tubes No.1, 2 and 4
Fine sponge
Board edge ribbon

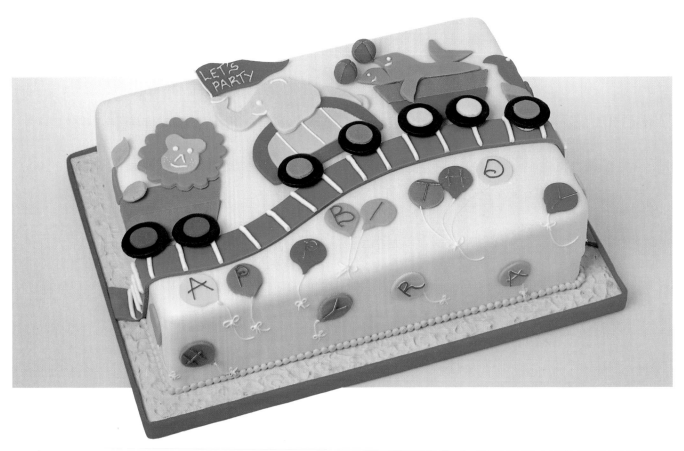

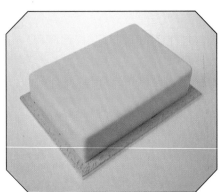

1 Cover the cake with sugarpaste. Then stipple the board with royal icing.

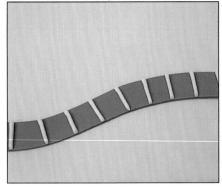

2 Cut and fix a sugarpaste track over the cake-top and sides. Pipe the lines with royal icing (No.4).

3 Using the templates as a guide, cut and fix an assortment of sugarpaste animals and carriages.

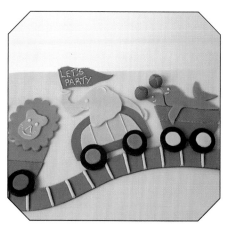

4 Cut and fix sugarpaste wheels.
Decorate with royal icing (No.1).

5 Cut and fix sugarpaste balloons.
Pipe strings and bows (No.1).

6 Pipe message on balloons (No.1).
Pipe shells around the cake-
base (No.2).

TEDDIE

INGREDIENTS

20.5cm round sponge (8in)
Small sponge 3 required, or
  swiss roll for ears and nose
680g sugarpaste (1½lb)

EQUIPMENT and DECORATIONS

28cm heart shaped cake
  board (11in)
Piping tube No.2
Fine sponge
Board edge ribbon

80

1 Using the template as a guide, cut out sponge for ears and face, then fix to the round sponge. Coat with butter icing and chill for 1 hour.

2 Cover the head and ears with sugarpaste.

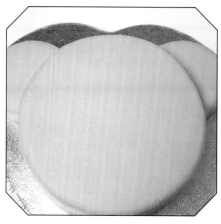

3 Lightly stipple with royal icing, using a fine sponge, to create fur effect.

4 Cover the face with sugarpaste and stipple with royal icing, then fix to the head.

5 Mould and fix sugarpaste eyes, then cut and fix the inner ears.

6 Mould and fix a sugarpaste nose. Pipe the mouth with royal icing (No.2).

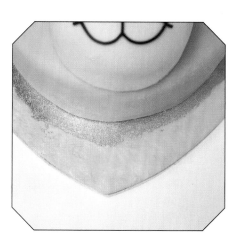

7 Stipple royal icing around the edge of the cake board to complete the decoration.

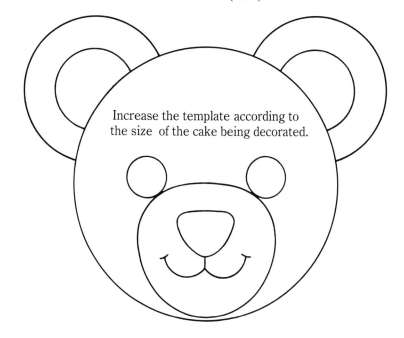

Increase the template according to the size of the cake being decorated.

CHEESE and MICE

INGREDIENTS

20.5cm round sponge (8in)
 2 required
1.25k sugarpaste (2½lb)
115g royal icing (4oz)
Assorted food colours

EQUIPMENT and DECORATIONS

35.5 x 25.5cm cake board
 (14 x 10in)
Piping tube No.1
Board edge ribbon

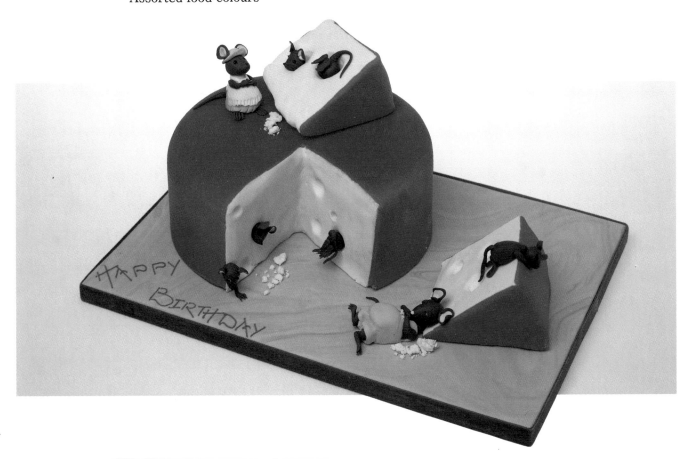

1 Cut two wedges out from the cake. Cut holes in the wedges and cake, then cover with sugarpaste to form cheese. Cover the board with sugarpaste.

2 Make and dress a sugarpaste father mouse. Make sugarpaste crumbs by rubbing sugarpaste between fingers and thumb.

3 Make and dress a mother mouse, then make the children. Fix to the cheese as shown. Sprinkle on sugarpaste crumbs. Pipe inscription with royal icing (No.1).

JEWEL BOX

INGREDIENTS

15cm square sponge (6in)
 2 required
900g sugarpaste (2lb)
115g royal icing (4oz)
Assorted food colours

EQUIPMENT and DECORATIONS

25.5cm square cake board (10in)
18 x 15cm cake card (7 x 6in)
Crimper
Piping tubes No.1 and 42

Decorative board covering
Assorted jewellery
Ribbon bows
Board edge ribbon

1 Cover the cake-sides with mottled sugarpaste. Cover the cake-top with sugarpaste and crimp edges.

2 Cut a thin card for the cake-top and cover with two layers of mottled sugarpaste.

3 Cut and fix sugarpaste pieces to front of the cake-side. Place assorted jewellery over the cake . Fix lid to the cake-top. Pipe shells around edge (No.42). Make and decorate a plaque.

JUGGLING CLOWN

INGREDIENTS

20.5cm round sponge (8in)
  2 required
1.25k sugarpaste (2½lb)
115g royal icing (4oz)
Assorted food colours

EQUIPMENT and DECORATIONS

25.5cm round cake board (10in)
Happy birthday ribbon
Piping tubes No.1 and 2
Board edge ribbon

1 Cut out sugarpaste pieces, using the template as a guide and leave to dry for 30 minutes.

2 Pipe lines with royal icing (No.1) and fix pieces together as shown.

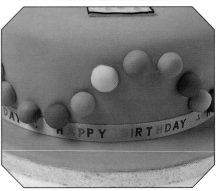

3 Fix the pieces to the cake-top. Make and fix sugarpaste balls, cut in half.

4 Pipe the line of loops (No.2).

5 Fix a ribbon around the cake-base. Make and fix sugarpaste balls, cut in half around the cake side.

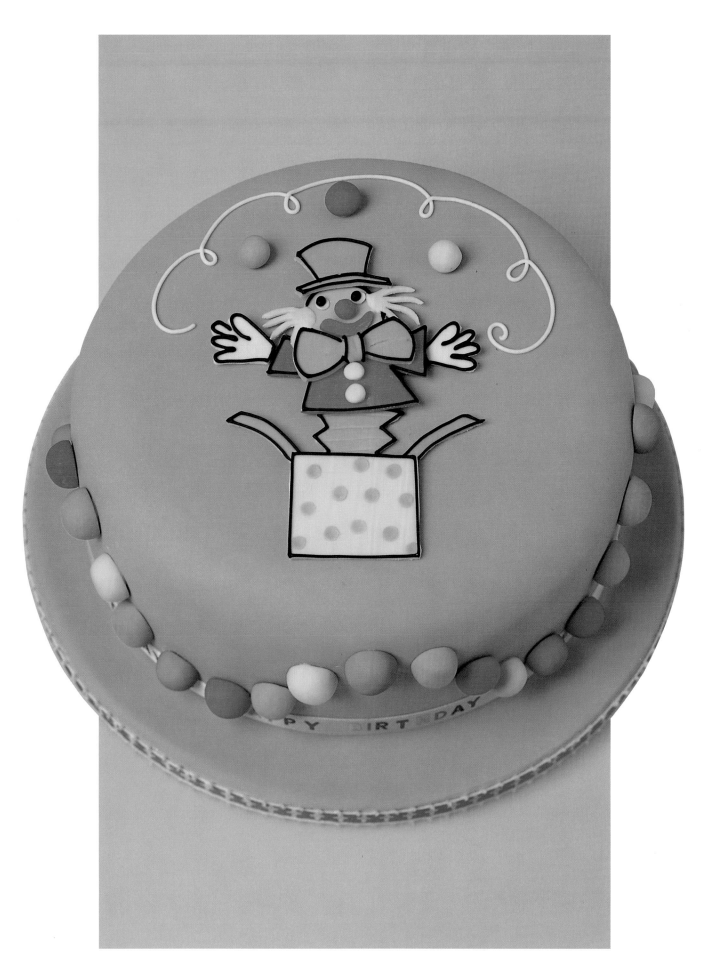

25.5cm petal shaped sponge
cake (10in)
1.5k sugarpaste (3lb)
225g royal icing (8oz)
Assorted food colours

33cm round cake board (13in)
Piping tubes No.1, 2 and 3
Fine sponge
Board edge ribbon

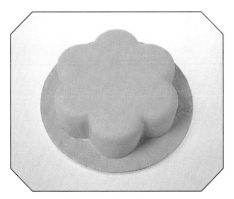

1 Cover the cake with sugarpaste, place onto the board, then stipple the board with royal icing.

2 Pipe the numerals as shown (No.2).

3 Cut out and fix sugarpaste shapes to form the face with the small clock hand pointing to the age.

4 Using the templates as a guide, cut out various animal and bird shapes from sugarpaste, or use shaped cutters.

5 Fix the cut-outs to the cake-side then pipe grass with royal icing (No.1).

6 Pipe inscription of choice around the cake board (No.2).

BURGER

INGREDIENTS

20.5cm round sponge
(8in) 2 required
1.5k sugarpaste (3lb)

Sesame seeds
Dusting powder
Assorted food colours

EQUIPMENT and DECORATIONS

25.5cm round cake board (10in)
Lettuce leaf
Gold doyley

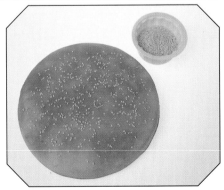

1 Slice sponge in half and cover the bottom piece with sugarpaste. Roll out sugarpaste and press against a lettuce leaf to create veins. Cut and fix with sugarpaste, beef burger, cheese and cucumber.

2 Cut out and fix sugarpaste tomato slices and onion rings.

3 Roll out sufficient sugarpaste to cover the top sponge. Sprinkle with sesame seeds, press them into the paste and cover the sponge. Brush surface with dusting powder and place onto the cake-top.

INGREDIENTS

25.5cm square sponge cake (10in)
900g sugarpaste (2lb)
Assorted food colours

EQUIPMENT and DECORATIONS

28cm square cake board (11in)
Decorative board covering
Cake card

Piping tubes No.1 and 2
Clown candle holders

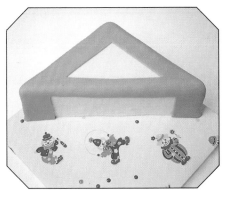
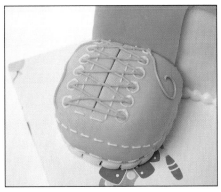

1 Cover the board with decorative paper. Cut the sponge across the diagonal, place onto non-stick paper or cake card, then position on the board. Layer and cover with sugarpaste as shown.

2 Pipe shells around the cake-base (No.2). Make sugarpaste trainers, stand on small pieces of cake card and fix in position.

3 Cut and fix sugarpaste letters as required. Fix clown candles.

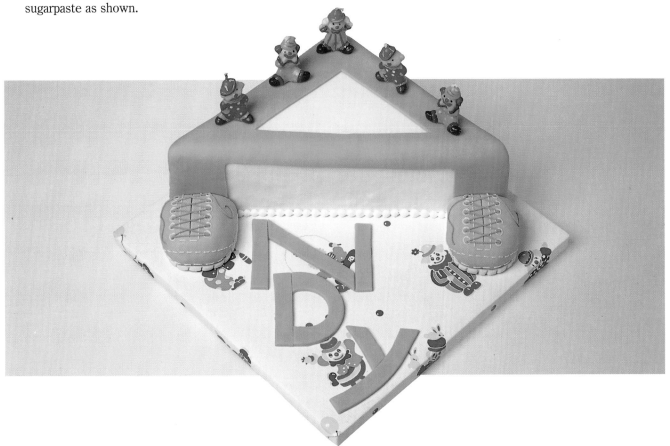

OUR DEVIL

INGREDIENTS

23cm round sponge (9in)
 2 required
1.5k sugarpaste (3lb)
115g royal icing (4oz)
Assorted food colours

EQUIPMENT and DECORATIONS

33cm round cake board (13in)
Piping tube No.2
Decorative board covering
Cake card
Board edge ribbon

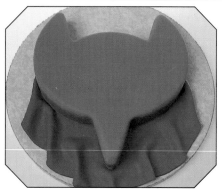

1 Cut the sponge, using the template as a guide. Assemble the pieces then cover with sugarpaste. Cut out a thin layer of sugarpaste and fix to the board.

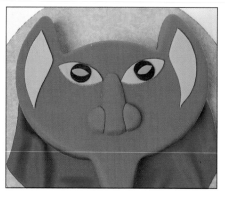

2 Mould and fix the nose then cut and fix the eyes and ears from sugarpaste.

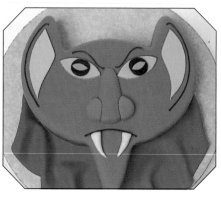

3 Pipe the lines with royal icing (No.2) then mould and fix sugarpaste fangs. Pipe inscription of choice (No.2).

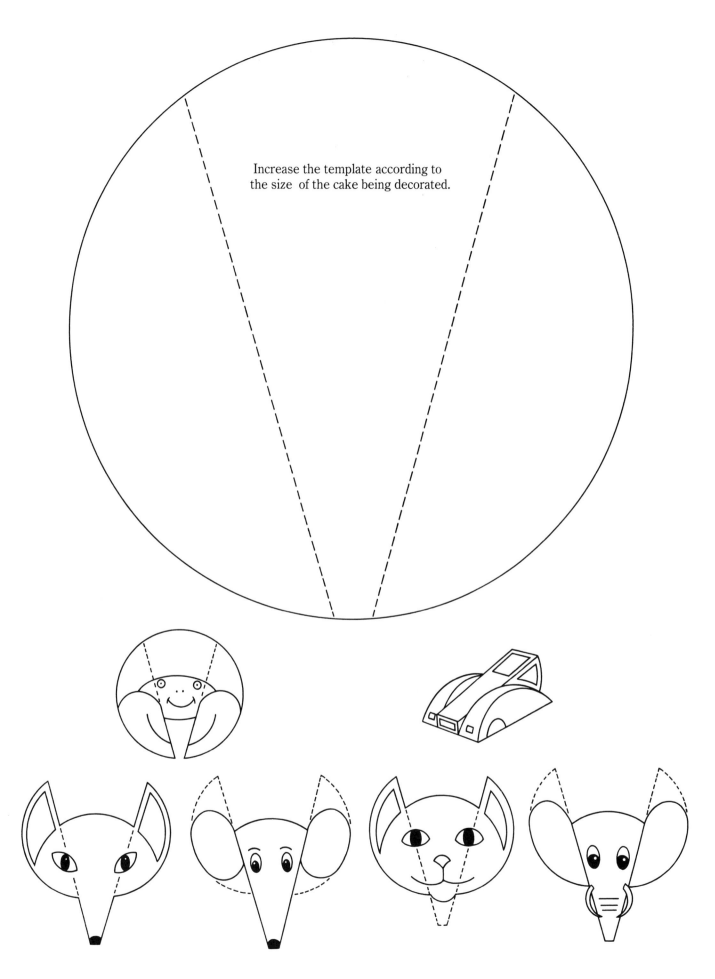

Increase the template according to
the size of the cake being decorated.

SWEET CUP

INGREDIENTS

15cm round sponge (6in)
  4 required
1.5k sugarpaste (3lb)
115g royal icing (4oz)
Assorted food colours

EQUIPMENT and DECORATIONS

30.5cm round cake board (12in)
15cm round cake board (6in)
Doyley
Piece of stiff card

Piping tubes No.1 and 2
Ribbon bow
Sugar coated sweets
Artificial blossoms

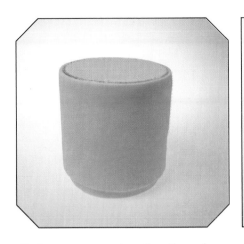

1 Layer sponges together then place a cake board onto the top. Trim and shape the base then cover the side with sugarpaste to the top of the board. Leave to dry.

2 Cut out a handle from stiff card. Cover both sides with sugarpaste and, when dry, pipe shells around the edge with royal icing (No.2). Leave to dry.

3 Cut out and fix sugarpaste figure and flowers as shown.

4 Carefully remove the cake board then cover the top with a thin layer of sugarpaste. Fix the handle with royal icing. Position on board and doyley.

Not to scale.

5 Cut out and decorate a sugarpaste plaque with royal icing (No.1) and flowers. Fill the mug with sugar-coated sweets and place some sweets on the cake board.

ALPHABET BRICKS

INGREDIENTS

23 x 15cm sponge cake
  (9 x 6in) 2 required
1.5k sugarpaste (3lb)
225g royal icing (8oz)
Assorted dusting powders
Assorted food colours

EQUIPMENT and
DECORATIONS

35.5 x 25.5cm cake board
  (14 x 10cm)
7.5cm square cake board (3in)
  4 required
Decorative board covering
Fine paint brush
Piping tube No.1

1 Cover the board with decorative paper. Layer the sponges together then cut into squares. Cover each square with sugarpaste, including the undersides.

2 Using the templates as a guide, cut and decorate sugarpaste letters and shapes as required.

3 Fix the appropriate letter and shapes to each cake. Assemble cakes as shown, placing bottom cakes onto cake card before placing on cake board.

DRAGON'S TEA PARTY

INGREDIENTS

20.5cm round sponge (8in)
 2 required
680g sugarpaste (1½lb)
225g royal icing (8oz)
Assorted food colours

EQUIPMENT and DECORATIONS

28cm round cake board (11in)
Crimper
Fine paint brush
Small edible flowers
Piping tube No.1
Flag
Board edge ribbon

1 Layer, then cover the sponge with sugarpaste. Fix to the board then stipple around the board edge with royal icing. Pipe leaves and fix flowers around the cake-side.

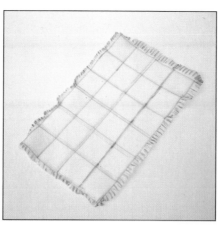

2 Cut out and decorate a sugarpaste picnic blanket.

3 Stipple the cake-top with royal icing then fix on the blanket. Fix additional flowers, as shown.

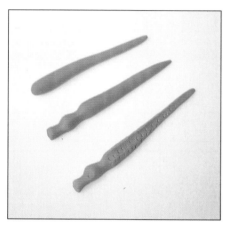

4 Mould sugarpaste into a dragon's body using the sequence shown.

5 Make wings, arms and legs using the sequence shown.

6 Fix the pieces together. Pipe the eyes with royal icing (No.1). Make a selection of dragons as required.

7 Layer colours of sugarpaste and cut into triangles for the sandwiches.

8 Make a selection of sugarpaste buns.

9 Make a sugarpaste teapot, cups and saucers. Fix all the items to the cake and board as required.

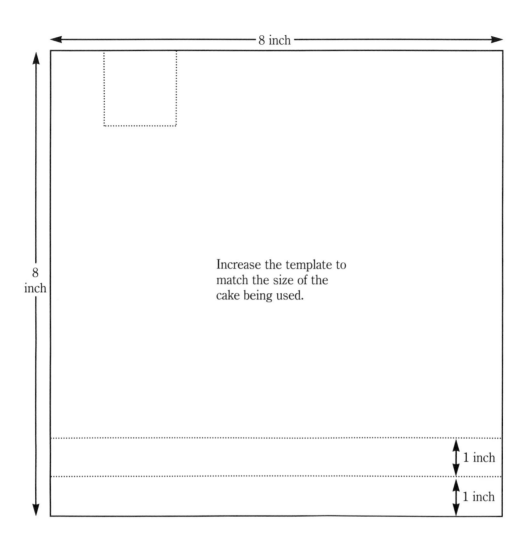

8 inch

8 inch

Increase the template to
match the size of the
cake being used.

1 inch

1 inch

1 Using the template as a guide, cut, layer and cover sponges with sugarpaste in an upright position for the engine.

2 Cover the sponge trimmings with sugarpaste, to form the two sets of wheels. Mark with the rule to form tracks.

3 Stipple the board with royal icing then fix on the digger. Sprinkle the ground with demerara sugar and coffee granules sugar.

INGREDIENTS

20.5cm square sponge cake (8in)
  2 required
1.75k sugarpaste (3½lb)
225g royal icing (8oz)
Demerara sugar
Coffee granules sugar
Assorted food colours

EQUIPMENT and DECORATIONS

40.5 x 30.5cm (16 x 12in)
  cake board
Rule
A piece of thick card
Assorted sweets
Piping tube No.2
Board edge ribbon

4 Make and fix various sugarpaste pieces to decorate the engine.

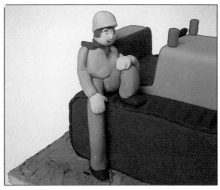

5 Make and fix a sugarpaste figure, as shown.

6 Using the thick card, make a shovel and fix to the front. Fill with sweets. Pipe inscription of choice with royal icing (No.2).

99

20.5cm round sponge (8in)
  2 required
1.25k sugarpaste (2½lb)
225g royal icing (8oz)
1 egg white
Coloured granulated sugar
Assorted food colours

28cm round cake board (11in)
Crimper
Fine paint brush
Piping tubes No.1 and 43
Candles
Board edge ribbon

1 Cover the sponge side with various colours of sugarpaste. Fix to the board then cover cake-top and board with sugarpaste. Pipe rope around the cake-base with royal icing (No.43).

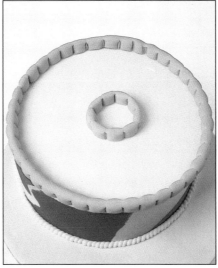

2 Roll out and fix two strips of sugarpaste to the cake-top, then crimp as shown.

3 Mould and cut a sugarpaste bumper car.

4 Make and fix trimmings, base and lights. Make as many cars as required.

5 Mould the various parts of a teddy bear as shown.

6 Fix the bear parts together. Brush with egg white and sprinkle on coloured granulated sugar. Make and fix as many as required. Pipe inscription of choice (No.1).

WATER SPLASH

1 Cut one sponge in half and layer together in an upright position. Cover with sugarpaste as shown.

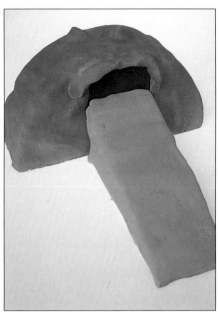

2 With the remaining sponge, cut to form slope and cover with sugarpaste.

3 Fix the sponges to the board. Stipple royal icing over the slope. Then stipple royal icing over the board. Make and fix sugarpaste logs onto the slope edges.

4 Make one whole and a half log boat with sugarpaste.

5 Make a selection of sugarpaste figures.

6 Fix the boats and figures as required.

INGREDIENTS

20.5cm round sponge (8in)
 2 required
1.25k sugarpaste (2½lb)
450g royal icing (1lb)
Assorted food colours

EQUIPMENT and DECORATIONS

40.5cm square cake board (16in)
Fine sponge
Fine paint brush
Motto
Palette knife
Board edge ribbon

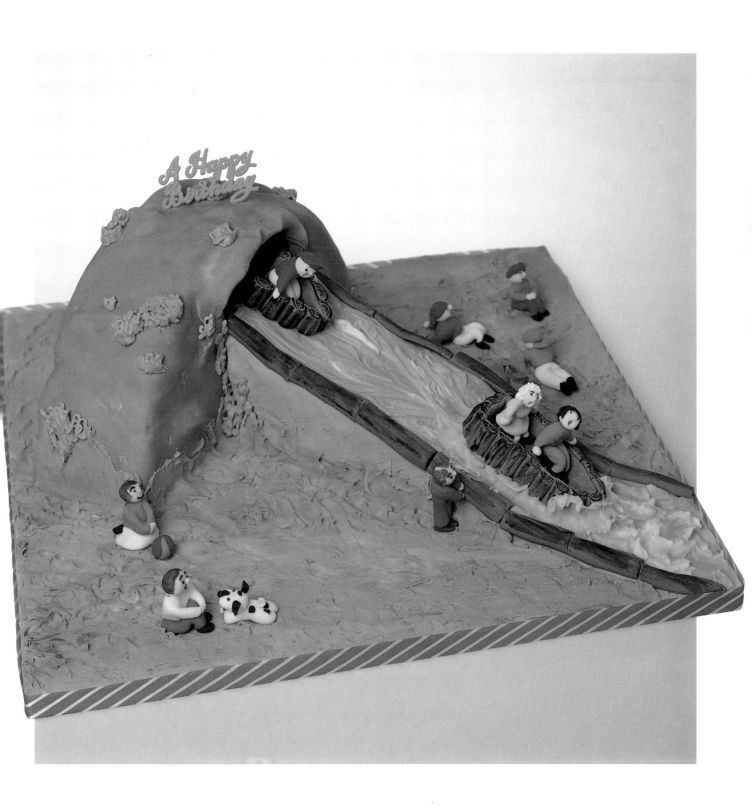

RIDING HAT

INGREDIENTS

Sponge baked in a 1.2Lt
pudding basin (2pt)
900g sugarpaste (2lb)

115g royal icing (4oz)
Black food colour

EQUIPMENT and DECORATIONS

35.5cm round cake board (14in)
Piping tube No.2
Birthday card

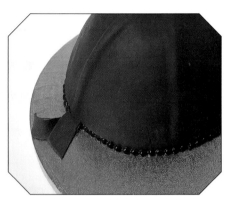

1 Coat the sponge with butter icing. Then roll out and fix six lengths of sugarpaste to form ribs, as shown.

2 Cover the sponge with sugarpaste and press down each side of the ribs. Cut out and fix a peak.

3 Cut out and fix a sugarpaste ribbon. Pipe shells with royal icing around the cake-base (No.2). Make a sugarpaste crop.

Vanity Case

INGREDIENTS

20.5cm round sponge cake
  (8in) 2 required
900g sugarpaste (2lb)
60g royal icing (2oz)
Assorted food colours

EQUIPMENT and DECORATIONS

30.5cm round cake board (12in)
Decorative board covering
Assorted cutters
Piping tube No.1
Board edge ribbon

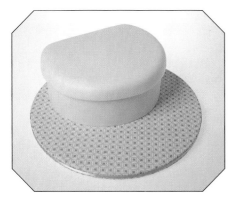

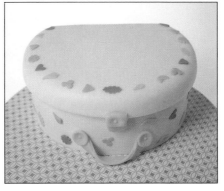

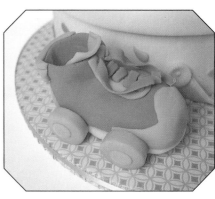

1 Cover the board with the decorative board covering. Trim the sponges to shape shown, layer then cover the side with sugarpaste. Cut out and fix sugarpaste lid.

2 Cut out and fix various sugarpaste shapes, handle and lock.

3 Make a pair of sugarpaste roller boots. Pipe inscription of choice onto the lid with royal icing (No.1).

105

MAKE-UP

1 Cover sponge and board with sugarpaste. Immediately cut the sugarpaste around board edge to form pattern shown. Then cut out and fix sugarpaste shapes around cake-side.

2 Fix ribbon around the cake-base. Decorate the side shapes with royal icing (No.1).

3 Mould and shape a sugarpaste head. Paint and decorate with food colours and dusting powders.

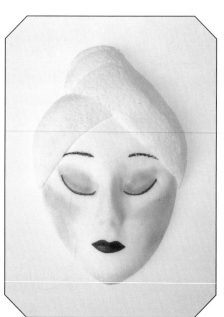

4 Make and fix a sugarpaste towel turban.

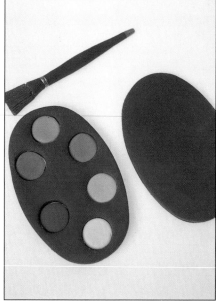

5 Cut out a sugarpaste make-up palette and brush set.

6 Fix the pieces to the cake-top. Pipe inscription of choice (No.1).

23cm round sponge (9in)
 2 required
1.5k sugarpaste (3lb)
115g royal icing (4oz)
Assorted dusting powders
Assorted food colours

30.5cm round cake board (12in)
Round cutters
Narrow ribbon
Piping tubes No.1 and 2
Fine paintbrush

MUSICAL BIRTHDAY

INGREDIENTS

20.5cm round sponge (8in)
 2 required
680g sugarpaste (1½lb)
225g royal icing (8oz)
Black food colour

EQUIPMENT and DECORATIONS

30.5cm round cake board (12in)
Piping tubes No.2, 3 and 43
Black narrow ribbon
Board edge ribbon

Increase the template to match the circumference of the cake.

1 Cover the sponge and board with sugarpaste. Pipe shells with royal icing around the cake-base (No.43). Fix ribbons around the cake-side.

2 Using the template as a guide, fix small sugarpaste circles around the cake-side then pipe the lines to form musical notes (No.2).

Increase the templates according to the size of the cake being decorated.

3 Pipe the stave (No.3) and musical notes (No.2) onto the cake-top.

4 Make and decorate a sugarpaste scroll (No.1).

5 Pipe inscription of choice around the cake board (No.1).

109

INDEX AND GLOSSARY

PIPING TUBES The diagram shows the icing tube shapes used in this book. Please note that these are Mary Ford tubes, but comparable tubes may be used.

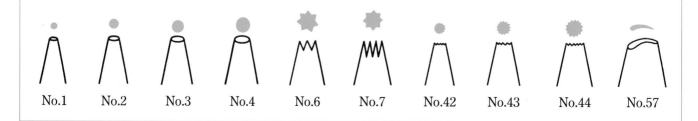

No.1   No.2   No.3   No.4   No.6   No.7   No.42   No.43   No.44   No.57

WHITWORTHS

For over 100 years Whitworths have been sourcing premium quality ingredients from around the world for people to use in baking and decorating cakes.

Dried Fruits, sourced from as far away as Australia and America, fall into two categories:

Dried Vine Fruits – Currants, Sultanas and Raisins are all made by taking whole bunches of Grapes from the grapevine and laying them out to dry naturally under the warmth of the sun. The resultant Dried Fruit is a source of minerals (including Calcium, Iron and Copper) and Vitamins, particularly A and B groups.

Dried Tree Fruits, are equally as nutritious as the Dried Vine Fruits. An extensive range is available offering the old baking favourites such as Dates, either sugar rolled ready chopped or whole, and Figs. Dried Plums, commonly referred to as Prunes, Apricots, Apple Rings, Pears and Peaches can be added in place of traditional Vine Fruits, to bake interesting cakes. Dried Banana Chips are great for decorating cakes or sprinkling over ice cream and puddings.

Glacé Fruits, are additional favourite store cupboard ingredients. Whitworths source only the finest Bigarreaux Cherries, grown in the Provence region of France and acknowledged to be the finest Glacé Cherries in the world.

Nuts play an important role in homebaking. In the past, Nuts tended to be used for their crunchy texture and flavour alone, but now they are recognised for their high nutritional value. Nuts are rich in Protein as well as Calcium, Vitamin B and Iron. All nuts must be stored in a cool dry place to ensure that they do not become oily or rancid.

The most popular Nut for baking is the Sweet Almond. Sweet Almonds are available whole blanched, flaked, chopped or ground and are ideal in cakes, biscuits and puddings.

Hazelnuts, sometimes called Filberts, are closely related to Cob Nuts. Either chopped or ground they can be added to cakes, pastries or puddings. The brown skins can be removed from Hazelnuts although the skins do look attractive when the whole nuts are used as a decoration.

Chopped mixed Nuts are handy for cake decorating and creating a crunchy texture for sauces and over ice cream.

Desiccated Coconut is produced by shredding the whitemeat of coconut and leaving it to dry in the sun. It can be toasted or coloured and used to flavour or decorate cakes or biscuits.

Using only the finest quality Almonds and Icing Sugar, Whitworths produce both Golden and White Marzipan to provide cake makers with an easy to use product for applying to cakes or modelling.

Whitworths were the innovators in the Ready-To-Roll Icing market, creating a delicious fondant Icing that takes the hard work out of cake covering. Unopened, the Icing will keep satisfactorily for months as long as it is kept in a cool place.

As an alternative to eloborate Icing techniques, a multitude of attractive ingredients are available under the Topits range. Multi-coloured Sugar Strands, Hundreds and Thousands, Chocolate Chips, Jelly Diamonds and Orange and Lemon Slices are just some of the prodcts that will bring fun and colour to cakes, ice cream and home-made desserts.

101 Cake Designs
ISBN: 0 946429 00 6   320 pages
The original Mary Ford cake artistry text book. A classic in its field, over 200,000 copies sold.

Cake Making and Decorating
ISBN: 0 946429 41 3   96 pages
Mary Ford divulges all the skills and techniques cake decorators need to make and decorate a variety of cakes in every medium.

Jams, Chutneys and Pickles
ISBN: 0 946429 48 0   96 pages
Over 70 of Mary Ford's favourite recipes for delicious jams, jellies, pickles and chutneys with hints and tips for perfect results.

Children's Cakes
ISBN: 0 946429 35 9   96 pages
33 exciting new Mary Ford designs and templates for children's cakes in a wide range of mediums.

Children's Birthday Cakes
ISBN: 0 946429 46 4   112 pages
The book to have next to you in the kitchen! Over forty new cake ideas for children's cakes with an introduction on cake making and baking to ensure the cake is both delicious as well as admired.

Party Cakes
ISBN: 0 946429 13 8   120 pages
36 superb party time sponge cake designs and templates for tots to teenagers. An invaluable prop for the party cake decorator.

Quick and Easy Cakes
ISBN: 0 946429 42 1   208 pages
The book for the busy mum. 99 new ideas for party and special occasion cakes.

Decorative Sugar Flowers for Cakes
ISBN: 0 946429 28 6   120 pages
33 of the highest quality handcrafted sugar flowers with cutter shapes, background information and appropriate uses.

Wedding Cakes
ISBN: 0 946429 39 1   96 pages
For most cake decorators, the wedding cake is the most complicated item they will produce. This book gives a full step-by-step description of the techniques required and includes over 20 new cake designs.

One Hundred Easy Cake Designs
ISBN: 0 946429 47 2   208 pages
Mary Ford has originated 100 cakes all of which have been selected for ease and speed of making. The ideal book for the busy parent or friend looking for inspiration for a special occasion cake.

Sugarcraft Cake Decorating
ISBN: 0 946429 30 8   96 pages
A definitive sugarcraft book featuring an extensive selection of exquisite sugarcraft items designed and made by Pat Ashby.

Cake Recipes
ISBN: 0 946429 43 X   96 pages
Contains 60 of Mary's favourite cake recipes ranging from fruit cake to cinnamon crumble cake.

Home Baking with Chocolate
ISBN: 0 946429 37 5   96 pages
Over 60 tried and tested recipes for cakes, gateaux, biscuits, confectionery and desserts. The ideal book for busy mothers.

Making Cakes for Money
ISBN: 0 946429 44 8   120 pages
The complete guide to making and costing cakes for sale at stalls or to friends. Invaluable advice on costing ingredients and time accurately.

The Complete Book of Cake Decorating
ISBN: 0 946429 36 7   256 pages
An indispensable reference book for cake decorators, containing totally new material covering every aspect of cake design and artistry.

The Beginners Guide to Cake Decorating
ISBN: 0 946429 38 3   256 pages
A comprehensive guide for the complete beginner to every stage of the cake decorating process, including over 150 cake designs for different occasions.

Desserts
ISBN: 0 946429 40 5   96 pages
Hot and cold desserts suitable for every occasion, using fresh, natural ingredients. An invaluable reference book for the home cook, chef or student.

The New Book of Cake Decorating
ISBN: 0 9462429 45 6   224 pages
The most comprehensive title in the Mary Ford list. It includes over 100 new cake designs and full descriptions of all the latest techniques.

BOOKS BY MAIL ORDER

Mary Ford operates a mail order service for all her step-by-step titles. If you write to Mary at the address below she will provide you with a price list and details. In addition, all names on the list receive information on new books and special offers. Mary is delighted, if required, to write a personal message in any book purchased by mail order.

Write to: Mary Ford,
            30 Duncliff Road,
            Southbourne, Bournemouth,
            Dorset. BH6 4LJ. U.K.